Stomping Ground

Published in the United States by

Beckham Publications

13619 Cedar Creek Lane, Silver Spring, MD 20904

ISBN: 978-0-9984870-3-8

Stomping Ground

Growing Up on the Streets of Greenwich Village

Dom Perruccio

With

Charles Messina

Silver Spring

"We're gonna stomp all night
In the neighborhood"
~*The Brothers Johnson*

DEDICATION

RINA ZAZZI - PERRUCCIO
Beloved Mother - Saint

These are the words that I carefully chose and had inscribed on your gravestone. God gave you a series of challenges your whole life, and you overcame them all. No one taught you how to be the perfect mother, being that you grew up without your own mother. You have always been an inspiration to your children. You were our rock, our safe place. You sacrificed your whole life for us. You were also a problem-solver and surrogate mother to my friends, and would treat absolute strangers in a kind and generous way. Your strength and fortitude were enormous.

When you died, my heart was broken. But I know that someday we will see each other again. Although your time here on earth was brief, your kindness and generosity impacted everyone you met. Life was better for anyone having known you. You were and still are my hero. May God bless you and keep you always in his heart as you are in mine.

V

Contents

INTRODUCTION
A Piece of Property

My neighborhood was much tougher than yours. Don't believe me, huh? I'll prove it to ya. Well, I can't really prove it, but I could make a case for it. The government made plenty of cases for it over the years, God knows. Madonna Mia! Isn't that what all these street stories are supposed to be about anyway: whose neighborhood had the toughest tough guys? Whose mean streets were the meanest of all? How do you even measure a thing like that? In fights won, years served in jail, in lives lost? What is the ultimate test for how tough a tough guy really is? I'm not sure. But I do know this, no matter how tough you think you are, there's always somebody a little tougher. No matter how tough your neighborhood is, there's a neighborhood just as tough, especially in New York City.

New York is all about turf. Nowadays, they call it real estate. Although it's nowhere near as real as the place I grew up in. In the Greenwich Village of the 1960s and 70s, it was called turf. It was your territory. If you wanted a piece of property back then, you didn't call Douglas Elliman. Ya took it by force. And if somebody ever tried to take over your territory, that was considered an act of aggression, an act of war.

New York is a city of neighborhoods. Some with real, old school nicknames, denoting the ethnic groups who first settled there, like Chinatown and Little Italy. Real places

1

with a history, and with people in them who built those communities and raised their kids and grew a life there. They gave breath and personality to what was just concrete and brick. Greenwich Village was a neighborhood.

At the end of the 1800s, the southernmost part of Greenwich Village, known as the South Village, became a staunch Italian enclave. Between the years of 1880 through 1920, well over 50,000 Italians, mostly from Southern Italy, from places like Naples and Calabria, settled in this area. These Italian immigrants, who were mostly poor and uneducated, occupied the previously uninhabited tenements and row houses that lined the streets of the Village. Before their bags were even unpacked, they started working; most of them in unskilled labor like factories;some of them ambitiously opened small businesses like shoemakers and butcher shops. They brought their work ethic, traditions, food, and culture to the Village streets, and they made it more than a place of occupied land. They made it a community.

For those of you who don't know, Greenwich Village is a neighborhood in New York City. But you knew that, right? The map says it officially runs north to south from West 14th Street to West Houston, and west to east from the Hudson River to Broadway. The area dates back to the 1630s when it was first settled by the Dutch, who named it Noortwyck. But like all turf, if you can't protect it, somebody comes along and takes it from you. That's exactly what happened when those bullies, the English, conquered the Dutch settlement in 1664. Eh, shit happens. Under the British, the area became a hamlet, or a Village, separate from the larger landmass of New York City.

The Greenwich part of the name seems to have come from a guy named Yellis Mandeville. He was a settler who bought a farm in the Village in the 1670s and named it after an old Long Island town called Greenwijck, which means

Pine District. I didn't know it either until I looked it up. That's how this piece of property of about 183 acres, and the setting of our story, came to be known as Greenwich Village. And now we know.

I'll leave the rest of the history to the historians, but one interesting fact from Greenwich Village's past is that New York State's first prison, called Newgate, was actually located on West 10th street, just off the Hudson River near Christopher Street; not far from the building at 95 Christopher Street where I was born and raised. Since the prison was north of what was the New York City boundary at the time, being sentenced to Newgate prison became known as being "sent up the river." That's where that term comes from, which is ironic considering how many of the people in this story actually were sent up the river!

Greenwich Village is traditionally known as a bedrock of bohemian culture. A neighborhood of colorful, artistic types and alternative, inclusive lifestyles. Some people might call them weirdos. These were my neighbors! Because of these so-called progressive attitudes, the Village became a hub for new movements and radical ideas. This tradition started during the 19th century and continued into the 20th century as newspapers, art galleries, and theaters located in the Village became popular.

In the 19th century, this exclusive area attracted famous poets, writers, and painters like Mark Twain, Walt Whitman, Salvador Dali, Jackson Pollock, Andy Warhol, William Faulkner, and Eugene O'Neill. They were all looking for some quiet place to create and mingle with like-minded individuals. In 1938, the first racially integrated night club in the city, The Cafe Society, was opened with black entertainers mixing with white entertainers. That place was way ahead of its time. In the 1950s and 60s, The Village attracted a counter-culture movement lead by those who became known as beatniks or hippies. They were seeking freedom from the establishment and rebelling against the government and against the society of the time, in general. Their causes were issues like free love, peace, and all things anti-establishment — drugs, politics, civil rights.

Greenwich Village gained even more of a reputation as an artists' enclave when the Beat Generation settled in. The Beats were a group of writers and poets who were rebelling against social conformity. The Village played a central role in the writings of Jack Kerouac, Allen Ginsberg, William S. Burroughs, James_Baldwin, Truman Capote, Maya Angelou, and Dylan Thomas. Off-off Broadway also began in the Village at this time as a reaction to Broadway and off-Broadway and as a rejection of commercial theatre.

In the 1960s and 70s, many famous artists including Bob Dylan, Jimmy Hendricks, Simon and Garfunkel, and Peter, Paul, and Mary started their careers in joints like the Village Gate, The Village Vanguard, The Blue Note, Cafe Wha, The Bitter End, and the Bottom Line.

Then, in 1969, the Stonewall Inn on Christopher St., my street, started a revolution when members of the gay community went up against the New York City Police Department for trying to close down the gay night club.

All of this was happening in the Village. The Village was happening. But the part of the Village's history that is less known is the part of the Village that I was from, the South Village. The South Village wasn't hip or cool or progressive, but it was ours. It was a working-class area of mostly tenement apartment buildings and small mom and pop shops, filled with Italian immigrants and first and second-generation Italian Americans. We were as much a part of the Village as anybody, and we had our own history.

The South Village runs roughly from West 4th Street and Washington Square Park on the north, to Seventh

Avenue and Varick Street on the west, Canal Street on the south, and West Broadway and LaGuardia Place on the east. Originally home to a merchant class, by the end of the 19th century, this area was dominated by immigrants, most of them from Southern Italy.

The Industrial Revolution started late and spread very slowly across Italy. While England was the first nation to industrialize in the late eighteenth century, the major industrial change didn't occur on the Italian peninsula until the late 19th century. Northern Italy went through the process first in cities like Genoa, Milan, and Turin. The industrial transformation resulted in the creation of the Italian nation-state. The northern political elite were responsible for this attempt at unification. This was a failed effort to unite people from diverse backgrounds and areas into one national identity.

But, by the late nineteenth century, many Italians still identified with their city, town, or village rather than with a national entity. Neapolitans considered themselves Neapolitans, Sicilians saw themselves as Sicilian, and so on. To this day, Italian Americans still identify themselves this way. They ask each other, "What are ya, Calabrese? Neapolitan?" It's a way of defining ourselves that harkens back to this time and place in our history.

National political leaders — dis-proportionately northerners — levied taxes and instituted a military draft, but neglected the needs of the population in Southern Italy. The Northern elite considered Southern Italians racially, biologically, and culturally inferior to those in the North. The neglect of Southern peasants, the scarcity of farming and other jobs, and the absence of government assistance caused a mass migration of Southern Italians out of Italy. Many of these Southern Italian migrants found labor opportunities in America.

From the 1880s through the 1910s, immigration from Italy to the United States was over 77 percent male. They came to America in search of work to help support their families back home. The years 1900 to 1910 brought more Italian men to the U.S. than any other decade in history. In subsequent decades, with the continued stagnation of the Italian economy, women and children traveled across the Atlantic to join the men. By the 1930s, entire families dominated these Italian-American communities in the United States. The immigrants from Southern Italy would ultimately create Italian enclaves in many U.S. cities, including New York. One area was The South Village.

These Southern Italian immigrants built their own distinct neighborhoods to distinguish themselves from their Protestant and Irish counterparts. By the late 19th century, Italians out-numbered the Irish in the Village, but were not sufficiently represented in the local church, the Parish of St. Patrick's on Mulberry Street, which covered the Catholics in that area. Not content with being treated like second-class citizens in their new land, the Italian-American community of the South Village built, with the help of charities and wealthy benefactors, the churches of Our Lady of Pompeii on Carmine Street and St. Anthony of Padua on Sullivan Street. Both churches still stand today as monuments to the poor but proud Italian parishioners of the South Village.

My maternal grandparents, Angelina and Marcello Zazzi were included in this wave of Southern Italian immigrants who came to New York City for a better life. Angelina and Marcello had two children, Rina, my mother, and Alfredo, my Uncle Freddy.

Angelina had an unfortunate life that was cut short by a stray bullet from a botched Mafia hit. It struck her as she walked down MacDougal Street. An innocent bystander in the wrong place at the wrong time. Sadly, I never knew Angelina.

Marcello was a beautiful man who lived well into his 70s and died of natural causes. He had his leg amputated later in life because of a stroke. I think heart disease runs in the family. It'll probably get me one day, too! Marcello knew who shot his wife, Angelina. He didn't say a word. He had no other family in America to help him raise Rina and Freddy. Marcello was no gangster. He was a hard-working man, a terrazzo mason. But he knew the code of the streets that were brought here from the old country. He kept his mouth shut; he did not go to the police. For his silence, the mafia brought his cousin Shana from Italy to help him with the children. They also gave him a financial reward. They put money in his mailbox every Saturday for almost 30 years. I know this because they would send me downstairs to retrieve it and bring it up. Every time he passed a mafia guy in the Village, they would tip their hat to him as a salute for being a "man of honor." It's quite a sacrifice to make—your wife's life in return for the respect of street guys.

My Uncle Freddy was "a man's man." Everyone looked up to Freddy. He grew up without a mother, survived the mean streets of the Village, and was drafted into the Navy as a teenager during World War II. He was stationed on an oil tanker escort, a very dangerous job, under constant attack from the enemy. He would cry himself to sleep at night. He survived the war but came back home filled with rage. If you crossed Freddy or rubbed him the wrong way, you would get the beating of your life.

He was one of the best street fighters the Village ever produced. Unfortunately, he made poor choices, got mixed up with the wrong crowd. He was arrested and convicted for truck hijacking, then again for gambling, which carried a prison sentence of four-to-12 years. The government wanted him to rat on his friends from the neighborhood in organized crime and to save himself. Freddy lived up to his reputation and the tattoo he wore on his forearm that he got in India during the war: It was a dagger with a snake wrapped around it with the words "Death Before Dishonor." He kept his honor, did his time, and came home after serving five years. Not long after, he died of a heart attack in his mid-fifties. The heart thing again. This family.

Then there was Rina, my mother, the matriarch, my idol, my love. Saint is written on her tombstone. Need I say more. She would give a stranger the shirt off her back. She sacrificed every day of her life for her family. She was cheated by life and died at the age of 66. I'll bet when she died and went to heaven and stood before the man, he apologized to her for the lifelong pain she had to endure. She was dealt a bad hand of cards. She also made poor life choices. The first poor choice was my father, Domenic. The second poor choice was Johnny the Bug. She had two children, me and my brother Vinny, who drove her up the wall at times.

Domenic Perruccio. My namesake. Dear old dad. His greatest accomplishment in life was that he never appreciated anything he had: a loving wife, two children, his extended family, and career-wise, he had his military record and training. What does he do with it all: he fucks it all up. As a young man, he worked for his father, Vincenzo, an accomplished tailor and clothing manufacturer in the family business. My father was drafted into World War II. He was trained in airplane mechanics, stationed in the Pacific, graduated up the ranks to Sergeant First Class. When the war ended, with his knowledge in training, and the advent of commercial aviation, he was set for life, right? What does he do? Does he go into aviation? He becomes a bartender! He wasted his whole life drinking, smoking, gambling, and died in his mid-70s. The only vice he did not have was womanizing. He was too self-absorbed and realized that women and relationships required work. And he did not like to work.

Italians love nicknames. Almost everybody had one in the neighborhood. My brother Vinny had a nickname that followed him for most of his life. Everyone knew him as Cooker. It was a unique name, to say the least. We had a cousin, also named Vinny who was born before my brother. To distinguish the two Vinny's from each other, my mother would call my brother "my little Cookie" in a baby-talk voice. The damn name morphed into Cooker and it stayed with him for 40 years, continuing to this day with all of our relatives and old friends. When we moved to New Jersey, he reclaimed his real name back. He is two years older than me, shorter than I am, but he was always smarter. He had better retention in reading and schoolwork than I did. My mother wanted him to become a lawyer. I think he could have done it if he wanted. Growing up, we had a lot of fun together and we also had a lot of fights with each other. But we were always loyal to each other. Brothers. Family.

This plot of land, this piece of property in lower Manhattan, with its history and its eclectic residents, became our home. We loved it there. We laughed there. We learned there. We learned the street code and the way of the world there. It was our world. It was unique to us. We weren't Bohemians or artists. We weren't Beatniks or hippies. We weren't gay. Heck, a lot of the time, we weren't even happy! We were Italians. Italian-Americans. We were Calabrese. Hard-headed and stubborn. And we came to the United States, in our case to the South Village, for a better life. We realized that sometimes things have to get worse before they get any better.

Chapter 1:

Members Only

Back in the day, my heyday, from the 1960s through the 1980s, I could have walked out the front door of my building at 95 Christopher Street and headed east on Bleecker Street, and I would have seen one familiar face after another. In those days, I knew everybody, everybody knew me, and we all knew each other. From the mom-and-pop business owners in the pizzerias, pork stores, and tailor shops, to the older men in fedoras and suits standing on the corners; everyone was local. They all gave me a warm hello, and they received one in return. The Village was a village in the truest sense of the word. It was a community, a small town inside a big city, a settlement.

"Dom, how are ya?"

"What's what, Dommy?"

"Dom, tell ya mother I sez hello!"

I couldn't go a block without a greeting. I recognized everybody and everybody recognized me. It was safe and insulated. Sure, there was plenty happening in the larger Village, but inside those streets in the South Village, from Christopher down to Canal, with Bleecker being the main artery running through them, was the domain of the Italians. It was our place, our rules, our thing. There was a way of being, talking, acting, and thinking. Either you understood that and belonged there, carrying yourself accordingly, or you didn't. Those streets, and that world, were known affectionately as "the neighborhood," and the neighborhood was like one big club. Either you were a member by virtue of where you were born and who you were with, or you weren't. There were plenty of smaller clubs, social clubs inside the bigger club. Those actually had signs hanging on the door that read, 'Members Only.' It seems like there was one on every block.

There was the Triangle Social Club at 208 Sullivan Street, which belonged to Chin. Dom the Sailor and Eddie the Blonde had a club on Sullivan too, but down by Spring Street on the backside of the park. On the Thompson Street side were Benny Egg's Club, Auggie's Cafe, and a regular SAC — Sports Athletic Club—not headed by a wiseguy, just a group of guys playing cards, shooting pool, and bullshitting. On West Broadway, right next to the cleaners before it became Bruno's Bakery, Lollipop operated an Italian SAC. Ciro had a club on Downing Street between Bedford and Hudson—basically a SAC, with drinks and card games. On Cornelia St. was the DeCurtis family club. With blacked-out windows, it never seemed to be open or to have any activity. Tommy Ryan had his warehouse on Jones Street for his jukebox business. The name of the business was Tryan Industries, and then it was changed to Gold Coin Industries. They had an office there. Jimmy Nap would visit sometimes. I know this because one day, Jimmy comes into Johnny's club and asks my brother, Cooker, to go with him in his flashy, white Cadillac. They drive over to Jones Street, where Jimmy gets out and asks my brother to circle the block until he comes out. Parking on that street was a pain in the ass. If a wiseguy asked you to drive his car while he was in a meeting, you went around in circles until you were dizzy if you had to.

Tony the Barber had Cafe Capri at 10 Morton Street. It was a hangout, but he did serve the general public coffee and drinks. The Bedford Club on Bedford Street operated as the Broadway Chauffeurs Club. Joe Marino's club was right across the street from the Bedford Club. Tweet was bookmaking there during the day, Perry and Dino were running the card games at night. Then there was Johnny the Bug (a lot more on him later) and Happy's Club on King Street, which had a big sign outside that read "Citizens for a better Village!" Happy was on the local planning and zoning board. All kinds of politicians came into his place: senators, assemblymen, members of congress, Joe Pepitone from the Yankees, and Johnny's associates from outside the neighborhood. All kinds of deals were going on there. You did not get your outside cafe approved unless Happy rubber-stamped it; he was an unofficial city official.

There were a bunch of storefront locations that were, in essence, private clubs or "fronts." Some of them would place toys and other stuff in the windows, pretending to be variety stores or junk shops, to make it look like a legitimate business, hiding the gambling, numbers, and swag.

Those were the main clubs. But honestly, the whole neighborhood could've had one big 'Members Only' sign on it, because no one from outside was welcome. If you were born there and hung out on the streets there, you knew the deal. You knew because you saw. You knew because somebody told you. And you knew because you knew; it was in your DNA. You can't teach somebody how to be from the neighborhood. You either are, or you aren't.

Inside the bigger club were the smaller clubs and cliques. The wiseguys had their joints. The old ladies had their church groups. Gamblers stayed with gamblers. Drinkers with drinkers. Housewives with housewives. And then there was our gang. Teenagers, Turks, Tough Guys, Jackasses! We were Jackasses long before Johnny Knoxville made it 'cool to be a fool.' I always considered our gang a group of intolerant storm troopers. We picked on anyone who was not us. Some in our group turned on each other. Denny broke a broom handle over Big Red's head, and then put his cigarette out in Mikey's ear. We teased each other to the breaking point, and sometimes somebody broke. We liked to think of ourselves as soldiers in Johnny the Bug's army. Johnny's Dirty Dozen. That's what he called us. We were his posse, his junior mob. We were his core, his inner sanctum. He enjoyed our company. He thought we were amusing. Sometimes Johnny would come to visit us at a local bar. He'd drink with us, then take us to a restaurant to cap off the night. He always picked up the tab. Ten or fifteen guys, drinking all night on Johnny's dime. It didn't matter; Johnny picked it up.

The Dirty Dozen line-up:

Johnny: Commander-in-Chief.

Dom: He called me "the brain" – type A personality, a thinker, an overachiever, a security expert, survivalist.

Cooker/Vinny: My brother, quiet, smart, liked cars and firecracker bombs, enjoyed card playing, sports, and gambling.

Vinny "Horse": Smart, secretive, strong, enjoyed card playing, sports, and gambling. Had an unusual ability to disappear, and make stinky farts.

Denny "ne-ne-ne": Sadistic, enjoyed excessive drinking and chain-smoking, bad friggin' breath.

Anthony "Big Red": Likes people, loved to coach sports, had a cult following in the neighborhood, his secret – he was an extremely giving person.

Tony "Augie" "brother 1": Loved wine, women, and song, enjoyed the good life, easy-going, and he was a big ball breaker.

Bobby "Tweet": Same as Augie, but throw in very smart in school.

Joey "Crazy Joe": Daredevil's personality, loyal, had the ability to adapt like a chameleon.

Mikey "Doorknob": Entrepreneur, enjoyed his beer, sadistic.

Charlie "The Chimp": Ability to climb like a monkey, big earner, had extreme street smarts.

Michael "Dippy," aka "The Pussy from Queens": Loved to fabricate stories, had an innate ability to embellish. In plain words, he was a bullshit artist.

This was Johnny's Dirty Dozen. Our antics, humor, and craziness were second to none. The gang extended beyond the dozen to include infamous neighborhood guys like Raymond Lopes and Rocco Arena. We were young and crazy and funny and dangerous, and we were protected.

A typical day for Johnny's Dirty Dozen involved hanging around the Bedford Club or Johnny's Club. We played sports; a lot of basketball, that was the neighborhood game. There were always girls. We were thinking about them, talking about them, chasing after them, sometimes fighting over them. Summer nights were spent in Leroy Street Complex, drinking, swimming in the pool naked, playing cards. We owned that park. By the time we turned 17 or 18, some of us, who had the foresight, went and found jobs. I had a construction job with Rocco Nap, Jimmy Nap's son, in Jersey City. Then I got a job with Diebold Safe Co. as a safe mechanic. Cooker worked for Con Edison. Johnny got him the job through Ray DeCurtis. Vinny "Horse" got a job as a Jr. Accountant. Denny worked for Zito's Bakery. Mikey "Doorknob" learned electric and HVAC. I got Charlie "The Chimp" a job with me at the safe company. Michael "Dippy," "The Pussy from Queens," had jobs in Queens. We had legitimate jobs during the week. But just like the movie Saturday Night Fever, we lived for the weekends. That's when we transformed into Johnny's Dirty Dozen.

The weekends revolved around bars like Dodge's on Bedford and Downing. That was one of our haunts. We started drinking in there at 16-years-old. The bartender, Little Philly, would serve us, no questions asked. He always carried a small gun. I guess to offset his diminutive physical size. He was in his 60s, 5 ft. 5 in., with a pencil-thin mustache. My mother and Johnny would drink with us there also. Dodge, the owner, was a good cook, and in the daytime, the patrons were mostly blue-collar workers from Varick Street, which, in those days, was the heart of the New York City's printing district.

Denny was drinking in Dodge's one night with a bunch of us, and decided to buy everyone at the bar a drink. Beer was 15 cents a glass, 25 cents for a mug, and we drank plenty of it. Then he says out loud so everyone can hear "except that Mexican," referring to a Latin-looking guy sitting on a stool. So, we keep on drinking, and Denny starts in again, "The only good Mexican is a dead Mexican." With that, the poor guy slammed his glass on the bar hard enough to break it. Then he walked out. Denny, like many of the guys, was sadistic and antagonistic. In the Village, physical and verbal abuse were give-and-take. We gave it; other people took it.

Then there was Tetley's Bar and Restaurant on Carmine and Bedford. Owned by an outsider, the place had a great atmosphere. Bedford Girls would hang out with us there. Kathy, Jackie, Maryann, Nancy. Auggie's parents would go there, and on occasion, Ralphie Gigante would pop in. He was friends with Dorothy, Auggie's mother. I think they went to school together. Hey, the way we acted out, it didn't hurt us to know more wiseguys. The waiter, a very colorful character, was named Joe Como. Joe was gay, and he was a great guy. He would make himself the butt of a joke before we could. By doing this, he controlled the situation and lessened the abuse he might have received. He was 5 ft. 8 inches tall, with a stocky build, a big black mustache and black hair that looked like a wig. He was a good waiter. He knew the business, knew the lifestyle, (his and ours), and went to the after-hour clubs the way most of the bar workers did back then. He always had entertaining stories. Joe lived in the Congress House on Houston and Sixth. He was murdered in his apartment; someone cut his head almost completely off. An unsolved murder. We raised a glass to him. Poor Joe. Rest in Peace.

There was also the Lodge Bar on Houston and Varick. This place had a pool table and shuffleboard. It was close to the Holland Tunnel, so Jersey drinkers would pop in. There would usually be a fight. There were a lot of fights. Like the night in Jimmy Maggie's on MacDougal and Houston when a bunch of outsiders came in, which was always a problem. A fight broke out and spilled over into the street. It was Cooker, Horse, and Denny and they were outnumbered. Cooker got cracked in the head with a beer mug, and needed 40 stitches.

The lighter moments in these joints involved Martini contests where the loser paid the tab. It was usually Denny vs. Big Red. Denny was a pro drinker. Red was a mountain of a man. They'd go at it, drink after drink. 1-2-3-4-5-6-7-8, and on the 9th martini, Denny would run to the bathroom to puke. Game over.

All of these bars would have the following patrons drinking with us: Jerry and Irene Vaughn, Bobby Genovese, Bobby Matavic, and Timmy Hanley. They were all heavy-duty beer drinkers, multiple quarts, wooden legs. Our gang was wound up enough when we were sober. When you added ethanol to the mix, we could become downright lethal.

In addition to the neighborhood bars, there were also gay bars in the West Village. The Mafia operated most of the gay bars in the 1950s and 60s, but none of us would ever go to these joints and vice versa. Places like the Stonewall Inn, the Ninth Circle, Uncle Charlie's, and later, the

Mineshaft, were blocks away, but they were a world apart. When some people think of the Village, they immediately think of gays and gay culture. It was a part of it. But it wasn't our part. And the two didn't really mix in those days. When they did, the results usually weren't favorable. Our group of guys would hang out in Leroy Park and Pool, which were a stone's throw from the docks area. The docks were where a lot of gay men hung out, looking to find other men to hook up with. The park at that time had a full-length basketball court, a great bocce court, which was fenced in and locked for the old Italian guys, six handball courts, and a blacktop softball field. The bleachers were massive and made of solid concrete. They were several rows high and they spanned the field from first to third base. They were modeled after the seating of a Roman Coliseum. We would hang out on the bleachers drinking, or in the pool swimming or scattered in quieter areas, making out with our girlfriends. Sometimes we would encounter some gay guys in the park, there for the same reasons. On occasion, they would follow one of us, mistaking us for one of their own. They could be very aggressive in their advances. That was something we didn't appreciate because we weren't gay, and we also saw any encroachment on our territory as an intrusion and a violation.

Charlie got it in his head one day that he wanted to teach one of them a lesson. He convinced one guy that he wanted to fuck him in the ass in the bleachers while the rest of us watched. The guy dropped his pants and bent over, and Charlie pretended to unzip his pants, but then took a long-neck beer bottle from his back pocket and shoved it in the guy's ass instead. We all laughed at this guy's humiliation and pain as he ran off frightened and, no doubt, badly injured, bleeding from the ass. In those days, in that place, this was what passed for fun.

One night we got word that a gay guy had been robbed in the park. He'd been stabbed, but managed to survive. Cops and detectives were all over the place trying to solve the case, and they were looking to pin it on us. They questioned our group, but we had nothing to do with it. Luckily, because the guy didn't die, it all blew over. Like a lot of crimes in those days, his stabbing went unsolved. The bottom line was that things were better off when our group and that group stayed on separate sides of Seventh Avenue.

Hanging out, drinking, gambling, fighting, and abusing strangers and outsiders was our pastime. We were young and stupid and carefree. Sometimes we were violent and nasty. In our minds, these were our joints, our streets, and our rules. We were a new generation of wild. Those who came before were protective of the area, just as we were, but they were more provincial. They were not rushing headlong into a changing world, facing the gay revolution following Stonewall, the rise of feminism, the civil rights movement, the counter-culture, and the explosion of the drug subculture into the mainstream. The world was changing rapidly all around us in the South Village, and holding onto the old way of doing things was becoming more and more difficult. Keeping our clubs, our lifestyle, and our neighborhood exclusive and insulated was a challenge that we were up for, though looking back, I see it was not one we were ever likely to win.

Chapter 2:

Johnny The Bug

Johnny "the Bug" Stoppelli was a highly respected member of the Genovese crime family. He worked for the infamous Greenwich Village crew, which was led in the 1950s and 60s by Anthony "Tony Bender" Strollo. Johnny was also my mother's second poor choice in men after the disaster that was my father.

I met Johnny when I was 10 years old. He came into our lives because of my father's enormous gambling debts. See, when you're a degenerate gambler like my father was, you borrow money from loan shark after loan shark. Pretty soon you're in way over your head; you owe multiple sharks an insurmountable and unpayable amount of money. Johnny "the Bug" had the capability to buy and consolidate debt from individual loan sharks. After all, no one was going to refuse Johnny.

For example, there was a guy in the neighborhood named Louie Malatesta. In Italian, his last name means 'headache.' Louie was in debt for about $100,000 which he was unable to pay back. So, Johnny, in order to protect his money, got Louie a union job with Local 3, the electricians union at Madison Square Garden. Louis went to work, and slowly but surely, paid the money back. It was a better resolution for both parties, because a dead man can't pay you back.

Johnny consolidated my father's loan, doing my old man a favor, because the sharks were no doubt going to hurt him. But it meant he owed Johnny a lot of money, enough that he'd be paying him back for many years. My father was under Johnny's thumb. In a bizarre twist of fate, Johnny and my mother began a relationship. I was too young to know the details of it all, and I'm not sure I ever really wanted to know. My parents' marriage was over, and they were legally separated before my mother and Johnny connected. My father was out of the house. And Johnny became a leading presence in our lives, and in our home, for many years. He was always around. I knew Johnny "the Bug" for 25 years, and yet, in all that time, I never really knew him. He was so diabolical and duplicitous that no one ever really could know Johnny. As a boy, I, along with the rest of my family, was heavily influenced, and tremendously damaged, by Johnny "the Bug."

When Johnny entered our lives, he was a stately figure in the mob. He controlled unions, gambling, shylocking, and the numbers rackets in Harlem, Brooklyn, and the Lower East Side. This was a more mature, established Johnny. It was the cleaned-up version of Johnny, a dapper, white-collar gent who had progressed up the ranks of the mob to become a man of great respect. The young Johnny was one of the founding fathers of the Genovese family. He started out as a crazed, vicious killer, a button man, working with people like Dutch Shultz in the Bronx. That's when he got the nickname "the Bug." In a business full of homicidal maniacs, you have to be a special case to earn a name like "The Bug"!

Johnny was an enigma. Police called him 'il Diavolo,' the devil. When they would follow him, he would seemingly disappear into thin air. Johnny was old school, he learned from the best and most notorious criminals of all time. He never once forgot his training or let his guard down. He was paranoid and trusted no one. This guy was on guard 24/7. That is why he kept his power intact and lived a long life, until he died of natural causes in his 80s. He saw many mafia Dons come and go. And by come and-go, I mean "murdered." He probably got his hands dirty on a few of those hits. No one really knew. He never discussed or bragged about anything. He was low-key all the time. When he walked down the street, he turned his head around so many times; it would make The Exorcist dizzy. In a restaurant, he stayed away from the doors and windows and always had his back to the wall. He'd had good training from "on-the-job" targets who had made mistakes, mistakes he had capitalized on. He put many guys to sleep, which they called "dirt naps." All the top brass knew his reputation. They respected him. Johnny was in prison only one time and learned from that experience. It was for murder. Legend has it he was released on a presidential pardon from Harry Truman.

Johnny's real name was Innocenzio Stoppelli, but there was nothing innocent about him. He was born in 1907 in Little Italy to Rocco Stoppelli, an electrician, and his wife Carmella, a cigar store worker. They were both Italian immigrants who married in New York city in 1900. As a teenager, Johnny formed a stick-up and robbery crew. He told police during one arrest that he was living off the profits from the hold-ups. In 1926, while living with his family in the Bronx at on East 216th Street, Johnny was arrested for the murder of Louis Bernardo in a pool hall at 108 Thomson Street. An associate of Johnny's, Peter Cinnamo, admitted to killing Bernardo in the fight and was charged with the murder. In 1938, Johnny was questioned following the death of a beautiful dancer named Thelma Giroux. Supposedly, Giroux leaped to her death from a fifth-story window of the Lincoln Hotel on 45th St. and 8th

Avenue in New York City. When the police came to the hotel to investigate, they found Johnny in her room. He had been dating Giroux for two years. Johnny told police that they returned to the room after a night on the town and suddenly, Giroux started ranting and raving and threatened, "I'm sick and tired of it all! Goodbye!" Johnny told the cops that he had left the room for a moment and when he returned, he found Giroux missing and the window open. The police bought Johnny's story and he was released. Giroux's death was eventually ruled a suicide.

When I met Johnny, he was about 55 years old, 5 ft. 7 in., 160 pounds, and partially deaf in one ear, compliments of a cop beating him on the head with a nightstick. He had also been shot once in the upper torso. At this point in his life, he was starting to bald, but he was always dressed sharply in a fedora, topcoat and suit. He wore a white shirt,and kept a hanky in his jacket pocket. He wore a gold watch with the face on his inner wrist. No other jewelry. Just gold and diamond cufflinks inscribed with the initials JS.

Johnny was in trouble with the law since his teenage years. He was involved in murder, and narcotics trafficking. In 1945, Johnny was directly linked to a multi-national narcotics ring. The business flourished from New York to California, importing heroin from Mexico. By the early 1960s, Johnny was said to be one of the most active, large-scale narcotics traffickers in the United States. He was a cunning, devious, dangerous arch-criminal, and he was an unpredictable maniac at all times. But he wasn't all bad.

Johnny liked kids and he loved animals. He bought us our first dog, a Boston Terrier, named Lucky. Lucky was likely named after an associate of his you might have heard of, Lucky Luciano. Johnny had the dog flown in from a breeder out west. On the weekend, when we saw him,

Johnny would bring home whole restaurant meals just for the dog. Johnny knew dogs were loyal and would lay down their lives for their owners. He respected that concept. He knew there weren't many people who would ever do the same. Believe it or not, Johnny came from a normal family. He had a sister and his brother who was an army colonel.

Having Johnny around also gave me instant street credibility. As I got older, he got me out of trouble many times. He went to bat for my brother and me, keeping us out of harm's way. It's hard to give Johnny an official title for what he was to us, but he was something like a common-law stepfather. Over those years, it was just my mother, brother, and me. On the weekends, Johnny would come over. To my mom, he was more than a boyfriend, and less than a real husband.

When you're living through something, it becomes your normal, even if you instinctually know something is wrong. Johnny, being in our lives, had its ups and downs. It had some practical benefits, and some real perks. In a neighborhood like ours, being associated with a man of his caliber made life a little easier on the streets. People knew Johnny was in our corner. On a personal level, though, something was amiss. He wasn't a fully committed partner to my mother. She deserved better. They claim that when you die, you stand in judgment before God and most sinners get chastised. I think that my mother got an apology! Johnny's lifestyle was touch-and-go and secretive. He was a phantom at times. He would give us stuff, and take us places, like the bowling alley at Sam Paladino's place near Sheridan Square. Johnny did more things with us than our biological father ever did. He would do nice stuff like that, but he wasn't a good influence at all. Johnny wasn't present in a real and lasting way. He wasn't a positive role model; he was a criminal. You can't have a criminal in your world for that long and not be corrupted by it. Johnny gave, but he also took. He contaminated our world.

In the end, a criminal only knows how to take. They spend every minute of every day figuring out how to make money, take money, make a score at all costs, no matter who gets hurt. Criminals like Johnny are narcissistic people who care about themselves more than anyone else. Their commitment to their life of crime comes above all else, and their crime family is more important to them than any other family.

We weren't Johnny's family, no matter how much we lied to ourselves and said we were. Our house wasn't his home. It was a place for him to hang his hat. Part of me wanted to be him; to have the money and the perceived power he had, to have the fear and respect he demanded from those in the neighborhood. The other part of me wanted to be nothing like him. The whole situation was screwed up and tremendously damaging to us all.

Chapter 3:

We Are The Champions

A kid growing up in my neighborhood back then had few choices. You could stay on the street, or you could stay in school. You could do nothing with your life, or you could do something. You could play with your balls, or you could play ball. I chose to play ball, softball, to be exact. I played in the CYO league, which was run outta Pompeii Church on Carmine Street.

Our Lady of Pompeii, St. Anthony's, and St. Joseph's made up the triumvirate of Catholic parishes in the Village. Each had its loyalists, and each had an elementary school attached to it. For over a century, these three churches educated and nurtured the spiritual growth of the next generation of Catholics in our neighborhood. From the outside, they may have all seemed the same. On the inside, there was a huge competition between the three, which made for intense intra-neighborhood rivalry. This competitiveness carried over to our sports teams as well. I was an Our Lady of Pompeii kid. That was where I went to school, and that was where my loyalties lay.

I also played basketball. Basketball was big in the neighborhood. It was an easy game to play—all you needed was a ball and a hoop. And it didn't cost anything. Each school had its own gym. St Anthony's had a really nice one, with a shiny floor, new rim and backboard, and an electronic scoreboard. Pompeii's was smaller and a little ramshackle. I don't even remember St. Joseph's gym. Basketball was a real city game because we didn't have the room for big football or baseball fields. We didn't have the money for equipment or fancy uniforms. Basketball's needs were minimal, which made it the perfect game for poor city kids. It gave us exercise and a sense of commitment and dedication. It also instilled in us a competitive streak. We wanted to win. We played with passion and pride, and when we wore our school's name across our chest, we took that seriously. Our schools were a stone's throw from each other, but on the court, we were worlds apart. Teammates were allies; opponents were enemies.

We had some good basketball players in the neighborhood and some real basketball wars at the Moricini Club on Sullivan Street against the Thompson Street boys. Our basketball teams were coached by Big Red and Johnny Pettinato, and I was an assistant coach myself. Johnny would go on to become the patron saint of helping young kids stay out of trouble. He founded a school, became the principal, and even went on to start the Greenwich Village Youth Council. Of course, like most guys from the neighborhood, he also found a way to have a problem. Even with the best of intentions, he got into trouble for letting kids with nowhere else to go stay at his house. That was a no-no. We had basketball teams with names like Magic People and the Dirty Dozen. The latter was taken from Johnny 'the Bug's' nickname for our group of friends. I still have some two and three-foot-tall trophies from our winning years.

In the summer months, the gyms would close. That meant the safe haven of indoor activities was gone. We had to hit the streets and the local parks for action. If winter was all about basketball, summer was all about softball. We played in the CYO, the Catholic Youth Organization League. As good as we were at basketball, we were just as good, if not better, at softball. I was the catcher on our softball team. I only wore a mask. I had no other padding, not even a cup. Somehow, I never got hurt. Ironically, many years later, in a Bar League, I was standing on the third base sideline, and a teammate let go of his bat while swinging. It hit me square in the face and pushed back one of my top teeth. I manually reset it. Six months later, I needed a root canal; the nerve had died. That's what happens when you get old. When you're young, you're durable. You can take the bumps and bruises and keep going. You're tough. We were tough. Our neighborhood was tough, and so was our team.

That CYO softball team was a squad for the ages. The first baseman was a lefty named Albert. He had a good, reliable glove. The second baseman was a kid named Kevin "Cool Cat" Martinez. His father was a longshoreman. And third base was played by Tommy Leo, an important player with good skills both in the field and at bat. Our outfield consisted of Harry playing left field, our big home run hitter, Steve Naglieri, in center field, whose father was a cop and who lived on Leroy Street in the same building as Louie Lump and Danny Sick. We hid Auggie in right field because he was spastic and terrible at sports. Our pitcher was the other Tommy, Tommy Borgie. And our shortstop was the notorious Rocco, Rocco Arena. Rocco was a good ballplayer, but later he would grow into infamy and legend in the neighborhood. He became a tough guy off the field; he was a drug-dealer and an enforcer for the mafia. He would turn into a malevolent bully who eventually met a violent end, but back then, he was just a decent fielder with a good arm. Our coaches were Anthony "Black Goose" Salustro, so named because he had darker skin than Stevie "White Goose" Masullo, and Artie Cooke. Artie's brother, Corky, was a loan shark who worked for Johnny and hung out at Happy's Club on MacDougal with Gazoot. But Artie was just a regular family man and a good softball coach.

This was the team. Talented. Tough. Tenacious. We may not have been the best team, but we wanted it more than the other teams. This was an early lesson in hard work paying off. This is the group that would become champions of the CYO league on September 28, 1972. The next day, September 29th, we were famous. We were all over the local papers—The Daily News, The Villager. We were all winners. That wasn't something most guys from the neighborhood could ever say. It felt good to be a winner, especially in a place where most young men were being groomed to be losers. Where easy money and the shortcut to respect came through crime. In this one moment, we were kids who did something meaningful, and we did it the right way. This was a life lesson that should have stayed with us and catapulted us forward to the straight and narrow. Unfortunately, for most of us, that would not be the case.

Chapter 4:

Random Acts of Unkindness

There is a certain amount of mischief and bad behavior that is simply a part of growing up. Kids do silly, stupid things without considering the consequences. They get themselves into trouble, and if they're slick enough, they get themselves out of trouble. As the years went by, the inglorious results of my misspent youth would become apparent. However, in the early days, when I was just a young jackass-in-training, before childhood high-jinks turned to sinister crimes, my misdoings were much more innocent and playful, except when they weren't.

If an idle mind is the devil's workshop, our minds were Santaland! The shenanigans all started in upstate New York. I was 8-years-old. My brother, Cooker, was 10, and our older cousin, Vinny, was 12. Every summer, my cousin's family would rent a house up in Narrowsburg, New York in the Catskills, close to Monticello, and we would travel up there to visit and spend some time. It was a great escape for us. Time away from the streets. A vacation. City kids like us, reared in concrete and tar, always looked at the country as a better life. Of course, the kids in the country always wanted the excitement of the city. Maybe you always want what you don't have. We wanted to see trees and run around in the grass and swim in clean water. Those summers in Narrowsburg were a welcome respite from the heat and grime of the city.

Our pranks started simple enough with things like price switching at Teglers, the local drug store in town. It was situated on a corner property off Main St. Across the street from Teglers was the Narrowsburg-Darbytown Bridge, which ran across the Delaware River and connected New York to Pennsylvania. This was the center of town. There were three or four stores, a gas station, a barbershop, and, of course, the drugstore. The owner of the gas station was Herbie Engleman and he was actually a Judge in town. That's the kind of town we're talking about. The town was like Mayberry from the "Andy Griffith Show." That's what it reminded me of. The only impression of country life that I had ever seen at that age was that show. The town was gentle and sleepy, with an untouched charm about it. It was nothing like the neighborhood that I was from.

Price switching was fun because it was a mild form of vandalism, for sure, but without really hurting anyone and it wasn't quite stealing. We were paying for the item, just the price we wanted to pay. It was like breaking chops without completely breaking the law. We would peel a sticker off of a lesser priced item and slap it onto a more expensive one. We weren't dirt poor, but I guess we just wanted more than our parents could or would give us. Price switching was a gateway activity to shoplifting. If paying less was good, paying nothing was better.

At this young age, no one would suspect me, Cooker, or Vinny of shoplifting. Especially no one in this small, gullible country town. To them, we just looked like three ordinary kids out to spend our hard-earned allowances on a toy, not three would-be thieves out to make a score. The front of Teglers drugstore had an old-fashioned ice cream counter. There were usually a few customers seated there enjoying a milkshake or an ice cream sundae. In the back of the store were the prized possessions that we had our eyes on—matchbox cars. Our plan of attack was simple. While one of us stepped to the counter and bought a car to distract the clerk, the other two would pocket a few more cars during the process and calmly and coolly walk out the door with them. Organized crime started here for us. It felt good to be bad, to get what we wanted, to outsmart adults.

Husco's Department Store in Pennsylvania was about a half an hour from Narrowsburg. In this store, we would switch prices on a twenty-dollar race car with something that only cost a buck or two. We would target the least experienced cashier and then roll the dice with our plan. Cooker and Vinny would send me to the register since I was the youngest and least likely to scam. So much for judging a book by its cover. At Husco's we raised our game to petty larceny. We would return home to Greenwich Village after a summer upstate, taking advantage of easy marks, feeling like our street smarts and guile could get us anything we wanted.

Back home, the corner of Bleecker and Carmine Street was our main gathering point. It was our little corner of the world and we defended it like it was all we had. It was our turf. Like Main Street in Narrowsburg, Bleecker and Carmine are where all the stores were and where life, in general, happened. Our Lady of Pompeii's basement gym was there and that was our indoor hangout. It was private, unlike the Leroy Street gym which was being overrun by Harlem outsiders. Big Red had convinced the Pastor to let us rehab Pompeii's basketball court, and we did the best we could with what we had, painting and fixing it.

Credit should go to Big Red, Me, Johnny Pettinatto, Tommy Borgie, and a few others who put in the time and energy to renovate the space and give us all a decent place to play basketball and to hang out. At the end of a night of playing ball, we would take the corner, eating pizza, or food from the Bar-Ba-Treat store on the opposite side of the church. Yoo Hoo was our favorite drink. I would drink one or two; Red would drink a six-pack. While hanging on the corner, we would abuse the tourist buses that traveled along Bleecker. Sometimes we'd yell at them; sometimes we'd give them the finger, sometimes Joey would drop his pants and moon them. We would also throw snowballs, eggs, or other more dangerous objects at them. That was a typical night.

The stores on Bleecker were owned and operated by mostly Italians selling their various products. Off the corner was the Margotta family peddling fruits and vegetables. One Christmas when I was 13, Big Red convinced them to let me and him sell Christmas Trees. We would buy them down the docks at a wholesale price and sell them at retail. I was a hard-working kid, always trying to make a buck, one way or the other. My mind was always in motion, and so was my body. I was always willing to do an honest or dishonest day's work. At that age, people in the neighborhood, even strangers, would hire you to do the donkey work: shovel snow, carry buckets of sand or stone from the sidewalk to their gardens in the back of their buildings. I had a lot of odd jobs, from food delivery and dry cleaners to cashier at the international food market on Sixth Ave. Back then, there were no scanners; it was all manual, so when I didn't know a price, I would let it pass by for free or I would put a low price on it, always in the customer's favor. It was my Robin Hood complex! I liked seeing working people catch a break.

When we weren't working or scheming, we also liked hanging out in Downing Street Park. This was a favorite spot of ours during the day. As you entered the park on the Carmine Street side, the walkway was between two buildings, perfect for modified stickball games. Rules and boundaries were set up years ago by the older generation before us. The pitcher stood behind the batter, and a strike zone was on the opposite wall, so when the ball is pitched, it comes back and the batter has the choice to swing at it or take a pitch for a ball or strike. When the ball was hit, it bounced back and forth between the buildings. You had to catch it before it hit the ground for it to be an out. If it hit three buildings, it was a home run. There was also the skeleton game that was on the floor. You had to flick with your finger at a bottle cap around this outdoor floor/board game, the first person to get to the skeleton had the power to chase everybody else and if their cap hit yours, you were eliminated. We would also play Wiffle ball. Over the fence was a homer. The park was dedicated to families, and you would see a lot of neighborhood fixtures there, like the Vaughns, for example. They were popular leaders in the neighborhood. I met Irene Vaughn there for the first time and she would watch us like a mother hawk in that park. We would tag our names in two places by hand with a paintbrush. This was early graffiti. Twenty years later, I could still read the names Chimp, Cooker, and Dom. I don't think that they're still there after fifty years, but I'll go check the next time I'm in the neighborhood.

At lunchtime, for a dollar or two, we had a choice of six stores on Carmine, and more than that on Bleecker, for cold cuts, hot sandwiches, or pizza. It's funny how years ago, with much less emphasis on health food and organic this and free-range that, things tasted fresher. Everything was a lot less complicated, and that alone just made it better. There was a certain simplicity and innocence beneath the insulated, provincial, racist, sexist, and criminal attitudes we grew up with. We also somehow enjoyed the simpler things, like a good sandwich or a summer day. Go figure!

The generation before us experimented with drugs more than we did, and so many of them became junkies, either killing themselves or someone else. We drank and smoked and fought and stole, but somehow we weren't plagued by drugs like other generations. We had a sense of pride in our neighborhood and especially in our church. We were proud of our Feast, which took place in July. We knew Our Lady of Pompeii wasn't the best or the biggest feast, but it was still ours. San Genaro was #1, Saint Anthony was #2 and we were #3. But we had something those feasts didn't have. We had a wider street. Carmine Street was a two-way street and it meant more room to walk through the feast and people weren't packed in like sardines.

Father Demo Square was a small triangular park across the street from Pompeii Church. It was named after Father Antonio Demo, a former pastor of the church, who had saved it when it was to be demolished. He was a great and dedicated priest to the community. All that kindness and history aside, the park was a good spot for us to bird-dog girls. Sorry to say this, especially in this day and age, but we were gropers. We would cop a feel by bumping into pretty girls going by. In return, we would catch a smack once in a while. And we deserved it.

On Sixth Avenue, we would fish for change that fell into the subway grate from the parking meters that were positioned over them. We used fishing line, a sinker (which is a lead fishing weight, about three 3 ounces), and a chewed-up piece of Bazooka Bubble Gum. We would put the gum on the bottom of the sinker, attach a line and bump the coin so it would stick, then carefully pull it up. I chewed so much gum back then that Bazooka Joe is still fucking me to this day! I have all my teeth and molars, thank God, but a lot of them are crowned. Some are time bombs waiting to explode to receive more crowns. I still remember Dr. DiStaci, the neighborhood dentist, drilling my teeth with a miner's helmet on. No wonder I never liked the dentist!

One day Auggie and I hatched a plan to "eat and beat" at Gill's Steak House on Sixth Avenue next to the movie theater. Gill's was attached to another restaurant, and they opened into each other on the inside. Our plan was simple: Eat in one place, run out the other one, without paying. It worked, except someone recognized Auggie, and they knew his father, Tony Black, who was a maitre d' at another joint in the neighborhood. We got caught. The next day we had to pay his father back for the check we tried to walk out on.

Another time Auggie and I had another brilliant idea. We bagged up dog shit and went to the roof of Mark Vierra's building. He was a classmate of ours at Pompeii. He lived on the top floor. Directly above his bathtub was a skylight. We found him in the tub one day and bombs away; we dropped the dog shit through the skylight and onto his head as he took a bath! He was pissed off and bigger than us, but we were fast runners and we ran to Tweet's older brother for protection.

Fireworks also played a big role in our jackass endeavors. We would light the explosives in building entrance ways to scare people half to death, and when we were feeling particularly destructive, we'd use them to blow up mailboxes. Being a troublemaker usually meant seizing opportunities as they presented themselves, and then acting fast for maximum impact. We did, however, also have bigger goals in mind. For example, we always wanted to break into the Food and Maritime School opposite Leroy Street Pool. One summer we were given the opportunity, or so we thought.

They were renovating the roof, and they had a Chicago boom extended out from the roof with a pulley wheel on the end of it. Six floors of heavy rope attached to a metal garbage can. Extremely dangerous and a complete violation of contemporary OSHA regulations. But back then, anything went. Our plan was to hoist someone to either the first or second floor, have them enter through a window, then have them come downstairs and let everyone else in through the front door. As we started to lift the first jackass, Charlie the Chimp, we realized this wasn't going to be so easy. We got him to the first floor, but the windows were locked. So, we hoisted him up a little higher to the second floor, the same problem. We lowered Charlie down and took a rest. We devised a Plan B. Plan B's are very dangerous. We decided we should hoist another jackass up, but this time to the roof. We needed a volunteer. No one stepped forward. Finally, Lopes said he'd do it if we paid him. We scraped together three dollars and fifty cents among all of us. It's a deal!

So, Lopes climbed in, and up he went. By the time we got him up to the fifth floor, we ran out of steam. And by we, I mean, five or six of us pulling at once. We started to let him down slowly, when suddenly the Devil entered all of our brains simultaneously. As we approached the third floor with him, this thought came into our heads, "Let's let go of the rope." And we all did! Well, except for Jerry Ottomanelli. He still held on to the rope to save Lopes from dying. Jerry received extreme rope burns on both hands for being a good and conscientious friend. We laughed our asses off. Lopes wasn't pleased with us, but strangely he wasn't as upset as you might think. He was just happy to make the $3.50! Lopes would do anything for money. He just loved money. He was an only child, not spoiled and not deprived. His penchant for the almighty dollar was unexplainable, and later in life, it would prove downright dangerous.

The Pier 40 docks along the West Side Highway were our version of Tom Sawyer on the Mississippi River. It was an adventure each and every time we hung out there. Going to the water's edge and feeling the breeze, looking at the passing boats and the unobstructed sunshine was uplifting to our spirits. We would smoke cigarettes or cigars there, fish for eel, shoot fireworks on the pier.

Occasionally, a boat was tied there. We would climb aboard it and imagine that we were sea captains. While on board, we would search the boat for any valuables that may have been left behind. Sometimes we would have "scumbag fishing" contests. It sounds disgusting, I know, but we improvised and invented a new sport. With a string and a bent hanger, we would catch floating scumbags - or what we called 'White Ghosts' floating along in the Hudson. If we happened to be with someone unpopular, they would get hit in the head or face with the scumbag. Sometimes we would haul one back with us and throw it in Leroy Pool. We definitely provided job security for the city employees who worked on cleaning up the park and pool. We broke our fair share of bottles in the park and set plenty of garbage can fires. Not to mention all the things we threw in the pool: scumbags, eels, sand sharks, and one time we stole fifty pounds of walnut powder from a truck and tossed that in the pool too. That one closed the pool for a day which was our intention. We were pains in the ass, ballbusters, and we loved causing problems.

If you weren't part of our main group, you would be the first choice to be pranked. Tommy Booth, who lived on Charles Street, decided to start hanging out with us. So, it was our duty to haze him. We're at Pier 40 one day, and we see a barge tied to the dock there. So, we board it and do our usual routine, searching it for valuables. This barge had a cabin below the deck. Right away, we hatch a plan to get Tommy below the deck so that we can leave him down there, untie the barge and let it go out into the river. It didn't occur to us that the Hudson is a major shipping channel and a runaway barge gaining speed with the current is potentially deadly. At around 4pm in the afternoon, we let it go with Tommy in it, and with us on the dock. At first, it's moving slow and he's screaming out to us for help, and we're all laughing our asses off. Soon it picks up speed and it drifts away and out of sight. We all go home for dinner, wondering if we're going to get a visit from the cops. Oddly enough, we don't. We're calling each other on the phone for any news, but nothing. The next day we found out that the coast guard rescued Tommy. The barge went out past the Statue of Liberty and was heading into the ocean. He could've been killed and the barge destroyed. All because of our adolescent antics and stupidity. In the end, we never got in trouble for it. Tommy never ratted on us. He also never hung out with us again.

Cafe Wha was a popular club, and Beatnik hangout on the corner of MacDougal Street and Minetta Lane. The front entrance was on MacDougal, and the business was in the basement. The emergency exit was on Minetta Lane, one flight up a set of concrete stairs. We would throw garbage cans, or sometimes bottles down the stairs and then run down Minetta alley to Bleecker Street for our escape route. The noise down there must have been deafening.

When we were kids, mass transit in New York City was 10 or 15 cents, and that included the Staten Island Ferry. Sometimes it was even free...if we didn't want to pay. Some days we would spend the whole day on the subway, going to Coney Island to grab a hot dog at Nathan's and go on the amusement park rides. On the way back, we would stop on 42nd Street, which was a cesspool back then, and buy stink bombs that were sold in packs of four or five. They came in small, sealed, two-inch long glass vials, each with a cap on it. There would be three or four of us on the train and the plan was simple: as we were about to pull into the station we would walk forward in a line, the lead guy would drop the vile onto the ground, someone behind him would step on it and break it. It took a couple of seconds to release its odor and then it took effect. We got off the train at that stop and would watch the reaction of the passengers looking around at each other thinking "who cut the cheese?!" If we had extra product when we came home, we would terrorize the neighborhood with it in stores. The rich people who had letter deposit slots in the entrance doors of their brownstones would get a stink bomb delivery. No one was spared. We were equal-opportunity chop breakers!

A more dangerous subway stunt was to put a coin on the track and have the train run over it and flatten it. We would do this at the 14th Street Path station, which was mostly empty, so we could go onto the tracks. This was not dangerous to the train but could have been to us. As usual, this became boring; we always had to experiment and move on to something more harrowing. So, we thought, let's put larger objects on the track, not thinking of the consequences. We tried bottles, rocks, all sorts of garbage and litter that was in the vicinity. Thank God we didn't derail any trains or get anyone hurt or killed, and perhaps even more important, we didn't get caught.

Chapter 5:

Johnny's Dirty Dozen

The Dirty Dozen is a 1967 film about a US Army Major who, during World War II, trains twelve convicted military criminals for a suicide mission to assassinate German officers behind enemy lines. They are a rogue bunch of loose cannons who take on a seemingly impossible challenge and get the job done. Johnny loved the movie and dubbed our group of jackass misfits 'The Dirty Dozen.'

Our Dirty Dozen nickname took hold in Lucy Jungs, a popular Chinese restaurant on Houston Street that we frequented. We would hang out in there, drunk and obnoxious, always on our worst behavior. There were a lot of us. We were from the neighborhood and everyone knew we were protected by Johnny. As teenagers, to have a made member of the Mafia as our mentor and defender made us feel strong and untouchable. We were young, arrogant, and seemingly indestructible. Nobody confronted us. They just let us be. If we were loud, we would stay, and others would leave the restaurant. If we were violent, the people we hit were the ones tossed out. We were always right, even when we were dead wrong. Nobody messed with us because nobody wanted to answer to Johnny. He had major street credibility. We were his proxies, his gang. We were Johnny's boys, his 'Dirty Dozen,' and we were about to graduate from pranksters to gangsters.

As we got older, the crimes we committed grew with our age. With the backing of Johnny and the umbrella he put over us, we felt shielded and safe from all responsibility and retribution, even from law enforcement. We did have parameters that Johnny set. As long as we did not go past those parameters, he would have our backs all the way. For example, if we were in a neighborhood scuffle, we knew we shouldn't drop his name. We were identified as the "Bedford Club" or Johnny's protected group. Most of the group would follow Cooker's and my lead, watching how we conducted ourselves. We learned from Johnny. He was not a man of many words, especially when he was in a group or in the club. His sidekick Happy, on the other hand, never stopped talking or joking around. Happy was animated. Happy was, well, kind of happy!

Johnny was more like Paul Sorvino's monster character Paul Vario in Goodfellas. The way Henry Hill describes him: "Paulie did not move fast, because Paulie didn't have to move for anybody." That was Johnny. You just knew, instinctively, just how far you could go. You could feel his aura, his energy, and if you had good instincts and street smarts, as most of us did, you knew when you could push forward and when to back down. On those rare occasions, when it was necessary to name drop in order to identify yourself, you went to him and explained the circumstances. You didn't wait for him to find out before you told him. This way, he did not get surprised or think you were hiding something from him.

This one particular Saturday, we got word that Chin was sending over Frankie Heart, a soldier in the family, to the club on King Street with Vinny to settle a dispute. Mikey, Denny, and Joey were pranking Vinny by phone. It got way out of control. On one call, somebody said to Vinny that they were going to dig up his dead mother and fuck her. That might have been going a little too far. That's when they showed up, looking for street justice. Vinny lived down the block from the Bedford Club. We always called him "Vinny the Creep." He was a petty chiseler and a conniver. Johnny immediately cracked Vinny in the face to set the tone of the meeting. It was an awkward situation for Frankie. Does he crack Vinny also? Johnny's slap was meant to send a quick message to Vinny, basically to say he was a guy who shouldn't be believed and who shouldn't come into Johnny's club to disparage kids that Johnny liked and trusted. It immediately discredited Vinny. After that, all we heard from Frankie and Vinny was, "Yes, John...yes John...yes John." We never heard what Johnny was telling them; his back was to us the whole time. When you went to a sit-down, even a minor one over something like a prank phone call, you never knew what the outcome would be. It could backfire very easily as it did for Vinny. After they left, Johnny walked over to us and said three simple but powerful words, "Cut It Out." That ended the harassment of Vinny. Johnny was like our very own twisted Father Flanagan, the good priest who founded Boys Town to help wayward kids. He was played by Spencer Tracy in the 1938 film Boys Town. Johnny was like that, only the opposite. We never wanted to disobey or disappoint him. In return, he was our bodyguard, our hero.

Another time there was a misunderstanding with this Jewish guy named Larry. Lopes was shylocking and lent him money. I would pick up the payments for him. One time when I was headed to meet Larry, two guys, Gary and Nuggie, appeared and confronted me. They were Ralph's men. They said, "Larry is paying us now." This basically meant, "Fuck You." I did not play the tough guy. I stayed calm and cool. I went to Johnny. We had a sit down with Chin's brother Ralphie at the club on King Street. The outcome was that Gary would collect the money for both of us, and I would go to the Carnegie Deli and pick up

Lopes' money. Ralphie told me at the meeting, "Next time identify yourself," meaning drop Johnny's name to avoid another misunderstanding. Sometimes the rules out on the street aren't that simple. You have to know when it's okay to mention somebody's name and when you shouldn't. I was young and still learning.

If you analyze our gang individually, you will discover that most of us were type A personalities and daredevils. We were raised in the street with a 'fuck you' attitude toward everybody. We didn't respect anyone, or any authority, except for Johnny. We were building a reputation as lawless, daring, and dangerous guys. We were Johnny's core, his inner sanctum. It was quite clear the reputation we enjoyed from our connection to him. What did Johnny get from a group of troublemaking teenagers? We made Johnny feel younger. We rekindled his youth. In us, he saw himself when he was a young, up-and-coming wiseguy. He also saw my brother and me as family. So, whenever someone came to him about our behavior, he would confront us to get to the truth, and then he'd go to bat for us. Often, he'd have to go to a sit-down on Sullivan Street with Chin or Ralphie. They'd ask him what had happened and he took the bullet. Whether he lied or stretched the truth or used his own influence and power to get us off the hook, we never really knew. But Johnny took care of it. He always took care of it.

In Charles Dickens' book Oliver Twist, the character of Fagin is described as a "receiver of stolen goods." He is the adult leader of a group of young kids whom he teaches to make a living through crime. He encourages stealing, pick-pocketing, and other criminal activities, and in exchange, gives the boys a place to stay. Johnny 'The Bug' was like Fagin to our Dirty Dozen. He encouraged our bad behavior: he endorsed it, supported it, and covered us for it. As kids who were raised with the morality of the neighborhood, we revered a man who gained power and respect on the street. We worshipped a criminal. Other kids had parents, teachers, and ballplayers as their role models. Mickey Mantle, President Kennedy, and Elvis. For us, it was a mobster. Just like Fagin, Johnny turned us into young hoods. He provided the boys with sustenance and safety, but in exchange, took their innocence away. He was our ringleader. He didn't hold a gun to our heads, but the fact that he had a gun, money, and influence made us admire him. It made us want to be like him. For some of us, he was the closest we had to a father. You could call Johnny an abusive father, but a father nonetheless. Abuse comes in different forms. Johnny never hit us and never threatened us. He never forced us to do anything. But, he was who he was. He had an impact on us, and on our development, and that was bad. It was negative and warped. A father's job is to teach a kid right from wrong, not how to do wrong. We were looking for guidance, support, and identity. Unfortunately, we were looking in the wrong place.

At the end of Oliver Twist, Fagin is captured and sentenced to be executed. The end is always bad for those who live a life of crime. There are only two real ways it can end, prison or death. When you're young, stupid, and desperate, you don't see it that way, or better yet, you don't care. Death and prison are things that only happen to other people, not you. You're smarter than they are. No one can catch you. The good outweighs the bad early on. There's easy money, the perceived respect, the camaraderie. Then, before you know it, you're Fagin, awaiting the death penalty and believing you're going to be smuggled out of prison to escape when instead you're going to be hanged.

Chapter 6:

Boys of Honor

In Italy, the Naples Mafia is called the "Camorra." The initial level of their membership is known as picciotto d'onore, or 'boys of honor.' Once a member proves his worth, as well as his loyalty and courage, he advances to the next level. That's what we were to Johnny. We were his "Boys of Honor."

We carried out many tasks for Johnny. Some jobs were menial, and others were more involved. We did a variety of things, from bringing the numbers the bookies took on the street back and forth to Christopher Street to driving him to Brooklyn to meet with Jimmy Nap. Sometimes we would drive him home. The drivers were always either me, Cooker, or Michael "Dippy" Di Pierri, aka "The Pussy from Queens." Dippy wasn't initially from the neighborhood. When Johnny brought him around, he introduced himself to us by saying, "Hi, I'm Michael Di Pierri, but don't call me Dippy." Wrong! From that day on, our group, being the major ballbreakers that we were, called him "Dippy." Then, one time, he cracked up his car when he was drunk and told Johnny a cock-and-bull story about how we were with him and he got jumped by an outsider and we didn't defend him. Johnny called us into the club wanting to chew us out. We were blindsided by Dippy's bullshit story, and when the truth came out, Johnny realized Dippy skunked him. This is why he gained the infamous and deserving nickname, "The Pussy from Queens."

In the beginning, Cooker and I partnered up on cars. We had multiple cars because we would buy cheap ones and get into car accidents, usually from drunk driving, then we would take off the plates and abandon the cars under the Brooklyn Bridge. One time when Cooker was arrested with Johnny and Smilie on West Broadway, they were in our second car, a 1966 white Buick Wild Cat. Blue interior, air conditioning, two-door, 455, 4-barrel carb, a fuckin' rocket ship. We bought the car from a doctor who lived in Auggie's building. But Dippy was worse than us; he would get drunk and get into accidents driving home to Queens.

Dippy would also borrow his father's car when he wrecked his own. A few other guys like Paul Christopher and Auggie #1 had cars but didn't drive Johnny. Johnny never drove himself. Once I asked him why he didn't drive. He told me that when he was younger, he had a partner named "Eddie Scar," and Johnny said one day he drove Eddie's Rolls Royce and wrecked it. I never asked anything further, and the subject never came up again.

The Bedford Club was located at 21 Bedford Street. It became our hangout, our meeting spot, our home away from home. On occasion, a lost limo would pull up, mistaking it for the 21 Club! It certainly wasn't. The physical size of the club was a challenge. It was one room, 20 feet wide by 35 feet deep. There was one sink behind the bar, and one narrow bathroom to the left of the bar in the back. The club was a hand-me-down from the older generation of guys before us who outgrew it physically and mentally. The rent was cheap, $150 a month. The building was owned by Mrs. Margiotta, Perry and Dino's grandmother. They were relatives of the Margiotta family on Bleecker Street with the fruit store. We had free electricity because, for years, the meter was in the club and not accessible to Con Edison, so they basically forgot about it. Or maybe somebody previously bribed the meter reader to take it out of the system. Cooker worked for Con Edison and developed many crafty skills to supplement his income. So, anything's possible!

The club started out with many members, then downsized to Charlie and me owning it and being responsible for the rent. Big Red was a big factor in Mrs. Margiotta trusting us and renting it to us. The size was somehow manageable because our parties spilled out into the street, and sometimes, we set the jukebox outside also. The cops rarely drove down Bedford Street. They turned a blind eye to our craziness. On rare occasions, when they received too many noise complaints, they would come and ask us to take it down a notch. On the weekends, in particular, I don't know how many of our neighbors even got any sleep.

When I was 14, I approached Johnny with two possible career choices for myself. One was boxing, to which he made a joke, asking, "What do you wanna box, oranges?" The second was a numbers store. He said no to that because of the high risk of misdemeanor arrests. I think he did not want to deal with my mother if I was put in harm's way or had to spend any significant time in jail. Although, over the years, he would ask me to do many things for him, from drug pushing to planning burglaries. Johnny was playing the part of the protector and also the instigator. He could be your best friend and counselor but also be a devil. He could lead you out of trouble and into temptation.

I don't know if any of us wanted to be gangsters. We grew up with it all around us. All of our heroes were bad guys. We even liked the bad guys in the movies. That's who we rooted for. In the world we grew up in, there were many good, hardworking, decent people who were going to regular jobs every day and breaking their asses to support their families. That was an admirable thing. It was a common thing. What was uncommon was seeing those working-class people with new cars, nice suits, jewelry, and the kind of respect the wiseguys had in our neighborhood. The age-old fear vs. respect argument notwithstanding, we knew what we saw with our own two eyes. At a very impressionable age, we saw guys who looked like they had everything. We saw how they were treated by other people in the neighborhood. We saw what we believed to be honor and respect. We wanted to be a part of that.

The one thing you don't see from afar is what it takes for a gangster to get to the point where he is perceived to be powerful, wealthy, and respected. The daily machinations of criminal life are difficult. They involve scheming, plotting, and deception. The criminal mind is constantly spinning. It has to be. The bottom line of a wiseguy's life is money. The great motivator for the mobster was greed. That is the place from which he derives his power. Having avenues by which he can earn. Earning is what makes a guy. That's where 99 percent of his brain power goes. Being a good earner is the most prized asset of any street guy. That means having ideas, having access, and having the balls to see it through. We were just a group of goofballs who liked breaking people's chops. We were about to find out if we had what it took to step up and be real street guys.

Chapter 7:

The 6th Avenue Demilitarized Zone

The neighborhood was split in half along 6th Avenue, separating the Bedford Street guys from the Thompson Street guys. The area of neutrality where each side could meet and mix without crossing into each other's territory was Houston Street Park. Houston, as it was called, was an oddly L-shaped playground with a concrete baseball field attached to a paved basketball court. You haven't lived until you've tried to field a grounder from a hardball off a cracked pavement. Guys from both sides spent time there. The park sat between MacDougal St. and 6th Avenue. It was right on the border. It was what was known as the Demilitarized Zone. I always thought of the high fencing around the park and along the avenue similar to the Berlin Wall. Both sides could gather and meet there in relative peace. Ass kicking wasn't prohibited but it wasn't encouraged either. It was also the staging ground for the annual fireworks explosions. I would say display, but sticking all the leftover illegal fireworks into metal garbage drums and setting them on fire isn't really something that rivaled the Grucci Brothers Macy's Extravaganza. The park looked like Beirut the next day. Houston Park was also the site of our annual Christmas tree burn. After the holidays, we would scour the neighborhood collecting trees, sometimes fifty or more, and set them on fire. The intense flames would rise above the height of the fence. The heat would also burn and damage the asphalt — our little way of saying 'Happy New Year' to our friends on the Thompson Street side.

On the surface, you might think the Bedford St. and the Thompson St. guys were basically the same. Both groups were young, Italian, and Catholic. We were both into sports and girls and crime. We actually had many things in common. There were also specific and important distinctions. Some guys could move freely between the two groups, like me, getting along with people on both sides and being able to hang out with both factions. I was born west of 6th Avenue, so that made me a domiciled Bedford Street Guy. But I had friends east of 6th Ave. and, of course, Johnny and Happy's club was on King Street, which was in Thompson Street territory. So, while the Italians of the South Village might have seemed like a monolith, an insider would know the differences.

A Bedford Street guy went to school at Our Lady of Pompeii; a Thompson Street guy went to St. Anthony's. A Bedford Street guy hung out in Leroy Street Complex; a Thompson Street guy hung out in Thompson Street Park. Bedford got pizza from Joe's or Golden Pizza; Thompson got theirs from Pizza Box or Ben's (there were actually two Ben's-one on MacDougal and Third St, and one on Thompson and Spring). Bedford wakes were held in Perazzo's funeral home; Thompson wakes were in Nucciarone's. Bedford had Faicco's Pork Store; Thompson had Raffetto's.

I can't think of one person who lived west of 6th Ave. who went to St. Anthony's. Was it the proximity? Did one block closer make that much of a difference? Was it legacy? If your father went to Pompeii, did that mean you went to Pompeii? Pompeii's structure was such that every grade had two separate classes. I'm not sure how the nuns in charge planned this or what their methodology was for dividing the classes. Did they do it academically, with one class being smarter than the other? I always thought my class was smarter than the other class. So, this actually created a rivalry within the same school! At times, I thought the nuns separated it geographically. Bleecker and Morton Street kids in one class, Christopher and Leroy Street in another. I'm not really sure. But even the perception of separation could cause friction and rivalry. In the later grades, this caused gladiator events during lunchtime. Our favorite place to fight was on Cornelia Street in the parking lot opposite the bakery. This lot was behind the movie house on Sixth Ave. This was our colosseum. Many pre arranged fights happened here. Also, the fight never ended, it would continue into the next day, sometimes the next week and beyond. I can't tell you how many times I fought Robert Gardella. He lived on Downing Street. I must have fought him at least ten times. Some days I would win, and the next day he would. The weird thing about it was, we never disliked each other. And when we went to La Salle High School, it was all forgotten. Although, he did make friends with Mocinno and DiLeo, two kids from the other side of Sixth Ave.

Another gladiator staged fight was with Marino Berkarich, who was in the other class. This fight started on Cornelia Street, ran out of time, and was finished in Leroy Park at a later date on a Friday night. He showed up, and we continued the fight. We were punching, wrestling, putting each other in headlocks, kicking. I swear this was like a marathon, with the older generation of guys and girls cheering on the fight. I said to myself, 'I can't lose this fight and show my face around Leroy Park again.' So, it got a little dirty. I saw a broken stick ball bat in one of those metal wire garbage cans. I grabbed it and whipped him with it. This brought a roar to the crowd and ended the fight. Marino left and went home; he lived on Minetta Street. It's ironic that we actually fought more with our own guys on our side of 6th Avenue.

I would cross the DMZ and go to The Morosini Boys Club, which had opened in 1938 as a place for underprivileged kids. It was a small but full and complete sports complex that had activities ranging from indoor pool tables to an outdoor sports area for summertime use. All age groups found activities to enjoy, and best of all, it was free. I would hang out with Charlie or Joey and sometimes even by myself. We would shoot pool, lift weights, and play pick-up basketball games. I was friendly with a lot of the Thompson Street Guys like Charles Villani, who would also shoot pool there. John Michael Bullaro was always there, so was Richie Aiello. I never got any bad vibes from being there with them. Fat Andy and Johnny Butch always kept everyone from fighting. Fat Andy lived on the east side. Johnny Butch was a Chin man, probably put there to intimidate us. He was a mountain of a man. His hands were so big that he could hold at least six pool balls in one hand. A Black guy named Lou was the basketball coach. The basketball wars that went on were unbelievable! Those fights on the court might've been more life and death than the fights off the court. And there were always lots of girls there which I loved. Playing basketball with girls looking on is one of the best feelings an adolescent boy can have. It was an opportunity to show off, giving it your best, caring how you look to others. It was an induction, of sorts, into manhood.

As far as neighborhood parks, Washington Square was a great place when we were young. It was a lot of fun for families, children, and students alike. That was before it was overrun by drug dealers, drug addicts, homeless people, and other assorted vagrants and miscreants. But it was too far away to hang out in as we got older. It was no man's land for Thompson and Bedford Street guys. If it had been ours, it never would've turned to shit, which it did. More on that later. Leroy Street Complex had a park, pool, gym, and even a library. This was the perfect hangout for us. It only had buildings on one side. Thompson Street Park was at a disadvantage not having the physical space and seclusion that Leroy offered. Also, a big advantage for Bedford was that we didn't have any wiseguy hangouts on our side of 6th Ave. We had gambling dens and neighborhood hangouts like our club, but no bona fide wiseguy places. They were all on the Thompson Street Side. With no clubs to contend with, we became the wiseguys; we owned the night.

Bedford crossed the DMZ on 6th Avenue much more than Thompson did. We even drove our cars there. Were we more adventurous and daring? Maybe we were just plain stupid. The only times I can remember Thompson coming over was for some parties at Teresa Marino's across from our club. I can say this; we enjoyed the Thompson Girls! This had to have pissed off the Thompson guys. Our favorite saying was, "fuck 'em if they can't take a joke!"

Over time we all seemed to realize that a neighborhood divided against itself cannot stand. We started going to the same bars. There were several along the DMZ, like Jimmy Mangia's. We also began to realize that a life of crime meant needing all the connections you could make. In the end, Johnny was the great equalizer. We went where he went. So, going to his club every day meant crossing the DMZ for me and for most of the Dirty Dozen. Everyone on the other side knew we were with him. They respected us. We were welcome there. It all became our neighborhood. We weren't outsiders. The real outsiders were our common enemy. Most people think outsiders were people of other races. That isn't necessarily so. While we didn't welcome anybody from outside the neighborhood with open arms, we had many more issues with other Italian kids from the

East Side, Fourth Ward, Uptown, Brooklyn, Queens, Staten Island, Long Island, and any place else that wasn't the Village.

In our Bedford group, and in our surroundings, we were exposed to people of various ethnicities. We had two Black kids in our clique. Ray Hennigan was one of them. His aunt owned one of the first Black businesses on Bleecker between Grove and Seventh Ave. It was called the Pink Teacup. It had a small sign below it that read 'Soul Food.' Ray worked with Mikey Doran at Chuck's food store on the corner of Grove and Bleecker. Chuck's store was a source of beer and cigarettes for us. Mikey stole everything that wasn't nailed down when Chuck wasn't looking.

Dallas Green was a Black kid in our group also. His father was the caretaker/janitor for the Hudson Park Library on St. Lukes Place and Leroy Street. He also had an apartment attached to the library, and that's where they lived. Dallas was older than us by about five years.

We had a full array of Irish kids on the Bedford side also Mikey Doran, Timmy Hanley, The Vaughn's, all full Irish, and loved to be Irish. Andy was Irish and Polish but never cared to be Irish. Joey was Italian and Irish but identified himself as Italian. Mikey Andriani was cousins with Timmy Hanley and all the other troublesome Hanley's, and he identified himself as Irish. We also had Irish girlfriends. I even married one! Kathy Gallagher. Her father was Irish, and her mother was Italian. Her mother's maiden name was Gaimari. Her uncle Johnny Gaimari grew up with Ralphie. I'm Irish by marriage! Everyone else in our Bedford group was full Italian. I think the problem with the Italian/Irish mixture is that it causes them to act double crazy! They are trying to serve two masters: the wildness of the Irish side, and the machismo of the Italian side. A dog can only serve one master or else you have to put it down.

The influence on the Thompson side was almost 100% Italian. The Italian American Civil Rights League was plastered all over the place in the neighborhood. Diversity wasn't their strong suit on that side. It used to be said that no one could walk down Thompson Street except people from Thompson Street. I saw guys kill each other on that street over parking spots. And they had the strength of Tommy Ryan, Benny Eggs, and Dom the Sailor, who all had clubs on the street. Thompson Street came heavy. You knew what they were about. If it was a heavyweight prize fight, Bedford was Ali, stick and move, and Thompson was Marciano, straight at you, brute force.

One fight that pitted Thompson against Bedford was the Jimmy Raisins – Dallas Green brawl. Jimmy was Thompson. Dallas was, well, I can't really say he was pure Bedford Street, maybe more like Carmine/Leroy Street. But for the purposes of this fight, he flew the Bedford flag.

The fight was announced days in advance. Jimmy was heavier than Dallas. Jimmy was the heavier puncher by reputation. Dallas was tall, thin, and athletic, so he was the better boxer of the two. I don't know who or why the fight was set up. Most fights just popped up out of thin air. This one was promoted. There was a lot of hoopla in the neighborhood in anticipation of the fight. Fight day arrived. Jimmy shows up with his Thompson entourage in enemy territory. The arena is Leroy Street Complex in the pool area. Like a lot of big fights, this was less than the viewing public wanted. The fight didn't live up to the hype it was given. This one was supposed to decide who was the better side, Thompson or Bedford. It ended up in a draw. They punched each other around. Nobody had a clear advantage. They both had boxing skills, so there was no wrestling, kicking, or dirty fighting like most street fights. They were evenly matched. Nobody was badly bruised or bloodied. Then the cops showed up and that was the end of that. I remember Jimmy leaving with his gang and the threat of a rematch, and both sides claiming victory. There never was a rematch.

A friend once said something must've been in the water on the other side of 6th Avenue. He could have been from either side of the street because each side would've said that about the other in those days. The reality is, we were drinking the same water from the same rusty pipes and the same old faucets (no bottled water in those days). And other times, we were drinking scotch and water. We were all in the same boat. Fighting for our little piece of the world that we lived in. Trying to survive in a violent, insulated, and at times, petty world. The streets didn't belong to us any more than they belonged to the hapless hippies and beatniks who walked around them. But we thought they did. We created arbitrary boundaries and borders to keep others away and to carve out our little piece of land. The same tactics that were used on the geopolitical level all over the world were happening right in our neighborhood. We had created our own invisible Maginot Line. The greatest separation was in our own minds. Once we realized that the things that made us the same were far greater than what separated us, we learned to get along and there was peace between Bedford and Thompson. It also helped that guys like us could be brought together in a cooperative way over such activities as bookmaking, fencing stolen goods, drug dealing, loansharking, and sports betting.

Chapter 8:

Chick Magnet

The wheel was invented around 3500 BC in Mesopotamia. I discovered it myself around 1964 in the South Village. A good way to get around the neighborhood in those days was on wheels. Bicycles, roller skates, and scooters were all popular back when I was a kid. This was before skateboards. I can remember the days of riding my scooter in Houston Park and around the entire square block, 6th Avenue, Bleecker Street, and MacDougal Street. That was my limit when I was young. Those were the boundaries. But I didn't mind. Round and round, I would go, in my own private Indy 500. I would scoot around with Charlie on my little metal store-bought scooter. Charlie had a homemade scooter, the type that was built with a wooden milk crate, a 2×4, and roller skates for wheels.

As we got older, we graduated to bicycles. We would go everywhere on our bikes. We'd ride them down to the ferry and go to Staten Island. We'd take our bikes on the train and ride in Central Park. Those first bikes were the traditional old-fashion Schwinn types. Later on, we evolved to the stylish 5-speed models with the chopper handlebars and banana seats. I had a candy apple red one. And, of course, the older I got, the more my wheels were used for one particular purpose: cruising for girls.

Around the age of 15, I partnered up with Charlie and Auggie, and we went to the Honda dealer on West Street down by the docks and bought a minibike. It had a yellow body with a black seat, a 49cc motor, 3-speed automatic, front and rear lights, and a kick start. Basically, it was a scaled-down version of a real motorcycle. It even had a key. It cost us 300 dollars. We chipped in 100 dollars apiece. The bike could fit two of us on it, so we took turns riding it. The maximum speed was about 30 mph with one person on it. We stored it in Charlie's basement, turning an old shower room into a hangout/storage room for Charlie and me. Charlie's father, Mario, who everybody called Larry Stretch, convinced the building's super to give us the room for free. Convinced likely means he intimidated or strong-armed him. Mario hung around with Anthony Huntz, a local shylock, and collector, and they both worked for and reported to Ralphie.

Bringing the bike up and down the stairs was a two-man job, so having a partner was a necessity. We were on a new level driving this mini bike around and showing it off to all the neighborhood girls. The bike also made us feel like outlaws, evading the cops when they would occasionally chase us. I don't think they were very interested in catching us, so we never did get caught.

In a span of about 5 years, we graduated from "Dennis The Menace" on scooters to "Hell's Angels" on bikes. At least that's what it felt like. I have to say we felt really cool with that mini-bike. It gave us a certain Marlon Brando in "The Wild One" kind of flair and swagger. Nobody in the neighborhood had that kind of a bike. Charlie the Chimp was Evil Knievel on it! He was daredevil numero uno. I was the second jackass. Auggie was in third place.

One day Auggie had a little fender-bender while riding the bike. The front wheel with the fork and shock absorbers was damaged. We brought the bike to the dealer. The repair job was estimated at 150 dollars, which was half the price of a new bike. We were upset that our chick magnet was temporarily out of service, and we also didn't have the money to pay to fix it. We left the bike at the dealer and told Johnny the story. Johnny's arms, extended by the tentacles of the mob, were far-reaching. A leg breaker named Gazoot, whose real name was Gaspar, worked for Johnny and hung out at the club.

Coincidentally Gazoot was juicing the owner of the Honda dealer. He was illegally lending him money at an unreasonable rate of interest. Gazoot convinced the owner to do the repair job for our bike for free. Gazoot was a mountain of a man. I'm pretty sure that he did not have to raise his voice to accomplish Johnny's request. Later in life, Gazoot disappeared from Johnny's club. We missed him because even though he was a big monster, he was always jovial and fun to be around. We asked Johnny and Happy, "Where's Gazoot?" They told us he was on the lam from the cops. We did not think anything of it. It was common for guys to leave town if there was a problem, and law enforcement might be looking for them. Two years later, the real story came out. Gazoot ran away with mob money, and they found his body in Las Vegas buried in the desert. Poor Gazoot. I liked him and he got our bike fixed. But he broke the rules and he had to go.

Some days we would use the bike to give the neighborhood girls rides. Nothing compares to the feeling of them sitting on the bike behind us, their pelvises pressed against the small of our backs. I'll never forget the feeling of them holding onto us around the waist; we were showing off, trying to scare them by speeding and popping a wheelie. It transformed us from jackasses to Romeos. It was intoxicating. Too bad we couldn't get them to sit in front of us and steer the bike. That way, we could slip our hands around their waists. We gave it the old college try anyway!

Eventually, I grew up, and I put away my childish things. I got rid of the bike. I got a car and gave the bike away to a friend of my Aunt Rose, a 14-year-old kid named Jackie DeRoss. We called him 'Little Jackie' because his father was 'Big Jackie,' who was an underboss in the Colombo Family. The bike went on to live another life of adventure in the exotic, far-off land of Staten Island.

While it was mine, that bike represented freedom. The freedom to ride and to go places, to leave the neighborhood when I wanted to and to come back was a great feeling. It was a mode of transportation, but it also transported my mind to a place of escape and openness. When you live in an area where people look alike and think alike, sometimes you need a little space to be alone with your own thoughts — a place where you can see different things and breathe different air. The bike gave me that. It gave me the freedom to have time away, with myself, with my feelings. When you leave a place, even for a short time, and then return to it, you have a chance to see it all anew. Whether that place is another street, another neighborhood, or another borough, getting away is good for the soul. My bike was good for my adolescent soul. And, of course, nothing was better for me as a teenage boy who was going through puberty than the attention of teenage girls. That bike was good for many things, but it was especially useful to my budding love life.

Chapter 9:

There's Always a Woman

In my neighborhood, there were rules. Most of them were unwritten; some were even unspoken. The trick to growing up the right way (or growing up at all!) was knowing those rules and following them. Another critical step was interpreting the rules. This was a particular skill because a miscalculation could lead to some bad consequences. Of course, careful manipulation of a rule at a young age could be tolerated and basically gotten away with.

Rules were all around me in the neighborhood. There were street rules, which were a learned code of conduct to keep you from getting killed or arrested. There were relationship rules, which taught you the proper way to treat a woman, such as a girlfriend or a wife. These did not apply to your mother. No one has to teach you how to do that, you just know. With other women where you have romantic relationships, there is much to learn. Rule number one, which I found in a fortune cookie at Lucy Jungs one night, is "Happy wife, happy life." I was there with Johnny, my mother, and a bunch of Dirty Dozen cohorts. I was 17-years-old at that time, and I should have paid very close attention to that fortune as if it were some kind of an omen. I was always popular growing up, outgoing, athletic, generous, and handsome, if I may say so myself! Talking to girls and having girlfriends was not a problem for me. Keeping those relationships was another story.

There were plenty of attractive girls my age in the neighborhood, on both the Bedford and Thompson side. One girl, in particular, was Kathy Gallagher. She had two older sisters. Kathy was the youngest. The middle sister was Helen, and the oldest was Mary Rose. Three gorgeous girls, one prettier than the other. The problem was, Kathy was going out with my friend Albert, the first baseman on my softball team. I waited for them to break up, then I asked Albert if it was okay for me to pursue Kathy. It may sound weird asking for permission but this was one of those honorable, unwritten street rules in the neighborhood that would help you circumvent hard feelings, violence, or possibly death. Albert gave me the okay and I was off to the races, courting Kathy.

When we started going out, I was about 16; she was about 14, so we basically grew up together, advancing into puberty and maturing through our formative years. This type of high school sweetheart relationship has a high percentage of failure due to adolescent immaturity and life inexperience. They used to call it puppy love. We entered this so-called puppy love relationship at a young age, learning as we went along and making plenty of mistakes.

At 16, I was already a ladies' man. I was all about giving chocolate and flowers, and as I got a little older, dinner, fine wine, and jewelry. Kathy was very generous with gifts and jewelry also. I was protective of Kathy because she was popular like me, and there were a lot of horny dogs in the neighborhood that did not follow the permission rule as I did. If one of these dogs got too close to her, I would beat the shit out of them. That's a simple rule also. This happened one day to a guy named Russell. He sniffed around Kathy and got a little too close. I drove him down the docks, beat the shit out of him and drove him back. I was used to street fighting. I had no fear and a lot of anger in me, especially when some scumbag disrespected me and tried to steal my girl.

Kathy and I finally moved to Saddle Brook, New Jersey, and lived together for a while. We got married on June 17, 1978. It was a wild wedding. Johnny, Happy and his wife Adelle, most of the Dirty Dozen, my side of the family (which are all nuts), and Kathy's side were all in attendance. We had that mixture of Italian/Irish culture all in the same room, drinking together, and getting crazy. Unfortunately, my fortune cookie advice, "happy wife, happy life, " didn't last too long, and the marriage dissolved. It was nobody's fault. We grew apart. It was more like the law of averages was against us, starting out too young. But I did learn the hard way from the failure of that marriage. I learned how to treat a woman and how to protect, provide for her, and allow her to feel supported and safe. Things you don't know when you're young and that can only be learned over time, with experience. The other Gallagher Sisters' marriages ended in divorce also, so maybe it was destiny for all of us.

Another rule was, "Never kiss and tell." This rule's meaning needs no explanation. It means what it says. It's the "omerta" code of relationships. You keep your mouth closed and you never talk about your sexual interactions. You respect the other person: their body, their mind, and their heart. Any guy who talks about that stuff to his buddies is an insecure jerkoff. If a guy started spewing that garbage in front of me, I'd say, "Would you like somebody talking about your sister like that? How about your mother?" That usually did the trick.

Life is funny. You never know what's around the next corner. A few years after my divorce, I came across an angel of a girl, a keeper, a beautiful person of Italian descent who was intelligent, sweet, charming, and pretty. I was a bit of an emotional wreck after my divorce, but I knew that life had to go on. I met Nina in a bar called Mando's in my town of Saddle Brook. I kept the apartment where Kathy and I lived after she moved out. Once Kathy was gone, I felt like a wandering cowboy on a lonesome trail, looking for companionship, searching for love. I was a wild Italian from New York. There is a difference between New York and New Jersey Italians as Nina and the locals of Saddle Brook soon found out. I would walk into Mando's club and buy all the blondes at the bar a drink. My favorite bartender, Gary, recognized me as a connected street guy. He went to after-hour clubs in New York and felt my aura from the first time we met. I would often drink bottles of Moet and I brought all this fanfare to the place because of buying all those blondes drinks. Gary started calling me "Dom Blonde." The funny thing about it is, I prefer brunettes! I married two, go figure.

So, getting back to my Nina, she was attracted to a bad boy, and that's exactly what she got. She knew that I was a big spender and that's what she got as well. I always showered my women with gifts as a token of appreciation and respect for them. I did not try to buy their love. I did not date gold diggers. They knew my generosity was genuine. Nina once said to me, "I noticed that you don't carry your paper money in a wallet." She was inferring that cheapskates tuck their money in wallets. Nina's family was well off but she was not spoiled and definitely not a gold digger. Lopes always hooked up with gold diggers, and consequently, his wife Gail ran off with a couple of millions of his cash.

Meeting Nina meant that my wandering cowboy days were over. The days of "Dom Blond" and drinking Moet were also gone. And so, the courtship began. I had to step up my game. I did not want to screw up this relationship. I was older and more mature. I had experienced a lot of things the hard way. I was still not totally recovered from my divorce, so I proceeded slowly with the romancing of Nina. I did my usual wine, dine, and jewelry courtship routine. This time around though, I upgraded the quality of the jewelry gifts. I had this bodyguard job in the diamond district protecting Charlie and Lopes. I tried to buy Nina the best that I could afford and the wholesale prices were fantastic. Diamond stud and diamond drop earrings, pearls, sapphire and diamond cocktail rings, gold watches, and gold everything.

But this was not what she wanted out of the relationship. She wanted the old "C" word, Commitment. Marriage, children, the house with the white picket fence, the American dream, she wanted all of it. It scared the shit out of me even thinking about all of this, especially having failed the first time. I avoided it like the plague. I was a knock-around guy, and I liked my freedom. Nina's father was protective and rightfully so, he told her to "Be careful with this guy; he might be stringing you along."

Nina gave up an opportunity to become an FBI agent because, as an agent, you could be stationed anywhere in the world. She felt that the commitment was one-sided. In work, as in her personal life, she wanted commitments to be both ways. Finally, and luckily, I came to my senses and proposed marriage. Thank God I didn't mess this relationship up and lose her. We're still married, and still happy.

So many guys in our world back then were cheaters and not committed to a one-woman relationship, even if on the surface they appeared to be. I was going against everything that I experienced being a street guy by committing to Nina. I believe you get out of life what you put in. If you give 100% to one person, you get 100% in return. If you put in 20%, that's what you get back. I had reached the point in my life where I was ready to give and wanted to receive

100%. We were married in the fall, October 8, 1983. The reception was at The Landmark in Rutherford, New Jersey. This wedding was larger than my first. Nina had a big family and her father had a thriving business with extended friendships. He paid for the entire wedding. The band had a singer named Johnny Sarno, whose father, Jerry, owned a coffee shop and was a shylock on Mulberry Street. Cooker was friends with Jerry. Little by little, I was being domesticated, reprogrammed back into normal life. It took 30 years to get to this point. I wasn't going to change overnight. Two children soon followed, Nicholas was our firstborn, and then Vanessa Rose. Family life was feeling complete.

By getting married and having children, I learned some things I didn't know before. One, I could break out of a cycle of stupidity that I had learned on the street and commit to something bigger than myself and that wayward lifestyle. When you grow up on the street with those rules and that way of life, you develop a warped sense of reality. Bad is good. Crime pays. Violence is the answer. It's a completely self-destructive and self-absorbed way of being. It's about taking what you can. Marriage and fatherhood are about giving.

The second thing I learned is that although the male lion is considered to be the king of the jungle, it's the female lion who is the better hunter/killer of the two. She tames the male lion's restless spirit. I also learned one other important thing: never juggle women. Juggling women is the equivalent of living in a house of cards. Sooner or later, the roof falls in on you and the whole house collapses. I never saw anyone get away with it. The truth always surfaces. Commitment to one woman is a better way. When you grow up seeing the opposite all around you, it takes time to learn the right way. I saw Charlie, Lopes, and Johnny get caught juggling women and lose their main women who were the prize keepers. Nobody can get away with it forever. The fortune cookie was right, "A happy wife, a happy life."

Chapter 10:

Johnny on the Spot

When I was 12-years-old, and Cooker was 14, Johnny brought us to the hottest nightclubs in town. This was before the formation of Johnny's Dirty Dozen. Johnny was just getting acquainted with us and he didn't know any of our jackass friends yet. He would bring us to expensive restaurants and classy clubs. We'd meet famous singers and movie stars. This was a side of life that few kids our age would ever see. He was taking Cooker and me under his wing, preparing us for a wiseguy life, and teaching us how to be big shots.

On the weekends, usually Saturday nights, we would go out as a family to dinner: Johnny, Mom, Cooker, and me. Most of the restaurants were in the Village and were owned by Johnny's mob friends. We were treated well there. People were extra nice to us and we were made to feel special. Johnny made sure we had everything from soup to nuts. He always paid, of course. Even though they knew him, Johnny picked up every check and tipped very well. Big shots always pay and always over-tip. We would rotate the order of places we'd go to so we wouldn't get bored with one particular spot. On occasion, we would hop a cab and go to famous places outside of the neighborhood, Uptown, or we would head east to Little Italy and dine there.

One spot east of the Village was "Sammy's Bowery Follies" at 267 Bowery. It opened in 1934 as a saloon in that run-down neighborhood known as 'Skid Row,' catering mainly to the homeless, the penniless, and the generally down and out. Life Magazine described Sammy's Bowery Follies as an "alcoholic haven." Years later, Sammy's changed its image and its name to the "Stork Club of the Bowery," after a surprising customer passed through: a monocle-wearing gentleman who was a British Lord. He had become tired of the fussy formality of the uptown clubs, so he decided to give the Bowery a try. Sammy's had now become a popular upscale cabaret. Fancy folks, tourists, politicians, and celebrities began frequenting Sammy's, looking for a place to loosen their ties, let their hair down, and slum it a little bit. It became common to find a socialite in an elegant gown nestled between a sailor on leave and an out-of-commission drunken bum.

It was a raucous place with an odd mixture of clientele, from the vaudeville performers on the stage, the social elite, and the Bowery bums brought in for atmosphere. I was not very impressed with Sammy's, although at that age, it was a socio-economic education for us, witnessing some crazy sights, and we had a lot of laughs there also. The place closed in 1970.

Another hotspot was the Copacabana. Everyone knows the Copa. Barry Manilow's song immortalized it. It's also depicted in all the gangster movies. Perhaps the most famous scene is the single tracking shot in Goodfellas, which follows Henry Hill's entrance, avoiding a long line and moving through the side door and into the club for a front-row seat. The Copa opened in November of 1940 and although Monte Proser's name was on the lease, it was rumored to be controlled by his partner, mob boss Frank Costello who had a frontman in the place that ran it named Jules Podell from 1950 to 1973. Proser was considered a well-connected nightclub owner who had acquaintances that included the likes of Walt Disney, Mary Pickford, and Maria Montez. Frank was out of the picture when I went there. He had been exiled from the mob in a power takeover by Vito Genovese.

Johnny was friends with Jules dating back to their 1930's bootlegger days when Johnny was a shooter, a hitman. When we went there, we received the VIP treatment and were greeted personally by Jules. We didn't bribe our way in through the basement like Henry Hill, we walked in the front door. Part of being a VIP, while tagging along with Johnny, included meeting the performers. I remember Bobby Vinton coming over to our table and signing a picture for me. I enjoyed this type of notoriety. I was being groomed at this age to become a gangster. The life-style was seductive. We were being taken to the best places, receiving the most attentive service, and were treated like royalty. Who wouldn't like that?

A similar hotspot to the Copa was the Latin Quarter in Times Square. It was opened in 1942 by Lou Walters, Barbara Walters's father, and it closed in 1969. This was another famous nightclub in which we received the VIP treatment. All the club owners knew each other and Jules's influence got us red carpet status in all of them. From the Latin Quarter, I have an autographed picture taken with singer Bobby Rydell. Now this place was

a particular interest of mine because it was filled with girls. Girls everywhere, girls galore! Scantily dressed. It featured chorus lines like in Las Vegas and an overhead high-wire act with these girls, half nude, swinging by. My brain mentally undressed the other half.

I'm happy to have had the opportunity to visit these places before they closed their doors. This era can never be duplicated again in history. Johnny would also come with us to places that were not so famous or fancy. He would go bowling with us or take us to a pool hall on the upper east side, a place called "The Chalk and Cue." In his own way, Johnny was being groomed too. He was being domesticated to become a family man. We were one big, happy, dysfunctional family!

Johnny liked taking us to all of these hot spots around town, perhaps just as much as we liked going to them. He liked being the man in charge and showing off his influence. He liked paying for things, throwing money around, and putting on display his big shot status for us all to see. He wasn't a showy man, or what anybody would call a show-off. But we learned by observing his behavior, what it meant to be a big shot. Johnny carried himself modestly and quietly, but his spending was immoderate and his influence was felt the minute he walked in the door. The way people flocked to him. The way other prominent people spoke to him and catered to him. Johnny was the man.

In any room we were in, he attracted attention and respect.

Drinks were sent over. People came over to see how he was, to kiss him on both cheeks. They asked how we were doing. People we didn't even know asked us how we were doing and what they could get us. There were extra cherries in our Shirley Temples. For a lifetime of murder, extortion, and racketeering, the real payoff, the final perk, the cherry on top for Johnny, was that the sons of his girlfriend would literally get an extra cherry on top of their drink. To us, at that age, that's what it really meant to be a big shot. Cherries. We hadn't yet found out about the pits. We soon would.

71

Chapter 11:

A Good Fella, a Bad Man

On the surface, Johnny was a sharply dressed, well-mannered, and respected guy. From a distance, you might confuse him with a 9-to-5 man, like an accountant or a stockbroker. Behind the scenes, in the den of his own social club on King Street, he was a shark. He had his hands in every illegal activity known to man, and with the help of Happy, his trusted sidekick, he was an influence-peddling force in local politics and beyond. He was a career criminal, a bad guy at heart who was looking to get even worse. But he was our guy.

It's interesting how your bad guy is a good guy until he's bad to you. You then realize being around him, having him as a role model and father figure is bad for you. The truth is, if you hang around with bad guys long enough, they will eventually corrupt you. Johnny did that to all of us. For every good thing he did for us, there was a price to pay, a debt, a bad act. Criminals like Johnny spend every waking hour figuring out a way to make money by lying, stealing, and conniving. It's in their DNA. It usually involves doing terrible, illegal things. These things have consequences. With Johnny in our lives, we suffered from multiple consequences. Simply said, he sullied our whole family from the day he entered our lives.

All the bonafide wiseguys in the neighborhood had their own clubs or hangouts that they used as bases of operation for their nefarious businesses, and, of course, as status symbols. Johnny's club was on the corner of King and MacDougal Street, across from St. Anthony's Elementary School. At lunchtime, the street was closed off and the little kids would run around and play, dashing between parked cars as they played Tag. Meanwhile, several feet away inside the green wooden facade and darkened windows, underworld figures gathered and conspired. This was the headquarters of Johnny The Bug. This is where he held court. He had his meetings there. He also did his plotting and scheming there. If those walls could've talked, hundreds of crimes could have been solved. It was a place where good and evil co-existed. Simultaneously, a place of beneficence and generosity and at the same time, it was the Devil's workshop.

The club is actually the place where I met Johnny for the first time. It was a brief introduction with Mom and Cooker outside on the corner — a fast hello and goodbye. I was just a kid, eight-years-old. The next recollection I have of him was our "family trip" to Florida. Exactly what family it was a trip for became obvious once we got there. Our destination was Miami Beach and the hotel was the newly-built Fountainbleu hotel.

This was my first trip to Florida, and it was memorable for many reasons, both good and bad. It meant Mom, Johnny, Cooker, and myself traveling together for the first time on an airplane. It was the 1960s and we were all dressed up for the flight. There were no flip flops or cargo shorts in those days. Mom had a sundress on. Johnny had on dress clothes and so did Cooker and I. Everyone was allowed to smoke on the plane back then; there were no TSA body searches, metal detectors, and no shoe exams. Flying was a way to travel in class and luxury. There was real food. We were served steak.

When we arrived in Florida and gathered our luggage, we were greeted by our driver, an old acquaintance of Johnny', whose name was Pigs. I kid you not, that is what we called him, and we never found out his real name. Being kids, we thought this was a really cool nickname, and we would ask him to make Pig noises. He was happy to oblige and amuse us by doing so! Pigs was a fun guy. An adult with a great, child-like sense of playfulness and humor. Much different from Johnny, who was stoic and usually had a very serious demeanor.

Thinking back, this was a quasi-business trip for Johnny.

A day or two after we arrived, Johnny met with Dominick "Dom the Sailor" DiQuarto. Dom was a capo, a captain, in the Genovese family's Greenwich Village crews. He was another type A personality sociopath like Johnny and like many other guys who held this important position. They tended to have big egos and when they didn't like one another for whatever reason, spent their time locking horns and measuring dicks! I remember the tension in Johnny's demeanor every time he mentioned Dom's name. Dom was the shakedown guy in Florida. Thomas "Tommy Ryan" Eboli, then the boss of the Genovese family, sent Dom down there to oversee their gambling operations. Florida was wide open to gambling since the mob was exiled from Cuba, and they wanted all they could get. Johnny had to meet Dom. That was the real family trip. We stayed there for about a week.

Pigs drove us around and showed us the town. Everywhere we went, we received the usual VIP treatment as wards of Johnny the Bug. I remember being poolside one day, and we actually egged Johnny on to dive into the pool. Some things and events in life are hard to forget, even if they are seemingly minuscule. Getting Johnny to dive in the pool was one of them. He never let his hair down that way, but this one time he did. Fun wasn't in his nature. He knew how to live and spend and how to live the high life, but otherwise, he was all business. We went home shortly after that.

Later in life, we became reacquainted with Pigs again in New York. He would drive us around just like he did in Florida, except we were now adults, and he would go to dinner with us. He was a friendly, fun-loving guy, even in his advanced years. Years later, Dom the Sailor came back to New York too. I guess it got too hot for him in Florida, and I don't mean just the temperature. His tour of duty for the family was done in Florida, and he set up shop on lower Sullivan Street near Spring Street. That was where his social club headquarters were located.

Another big part of Johnny's business was the numbers racket. It was a complicated operation, but it was a great source of revenue for him and for organized crime in general. Johnny worked with Jimmy Nap, who was the numbers king for the mob. Jimmy's operation was located in Williamsburg, Brooklyn. As Johnny and Jimmy Nap's business grew and they took on Harlem's action, my mother would be recruited to help handle the volume. She was doing the Lower East Side already with JJ as the controller, and Smilie was the controller for Brooklyn. They would drop off their slips at the cleaners every day and I would deliver them home to her. Mom would get home from work and start her second job, checking the numbers slips and producing the final tally slip that I would then return the next day. Every night Johnny would call to discuss the totals with Mom.

Mom was a pillar of strength and hard work. She could've been successful in anything she chose to do. She was always in the shoe manufacturing business. When she was doing the numbers in the evening, her day job was as secretary-treasurer of a company named Cels Enterprises. Their offices were in the Empire State Building. They had two lines of shoes called Chinese Laundry. One line was manufactured in Italy and one in China. They were sold in all the big-name stores in the country like Macy's and Lord & Taylor. Her gift of fluently speaking and writing Italian was necessary with the Italian part of the industry.

When she first started working outside the home, Mom had a different job on Bleecker Street, close to Broadway. She would walk there from Christopher Street every day. That kept her in great shape. That job was in a factory that manufactured shoes. It was a small operation; a basic office set up with just her and the owner. The factory workers were paid in cash. She would go to the bank for the payroll every week. One day she was robbed at gunpoint while returning to the building. This was pre-Johnny, and I was just a kid. She was unharmed. It was probably an inside job and she was likely set up by one of the workers. Mom was unflappable. The next week she went right back to the bank, alone. She was a tough lady and a dedicated mother to her boys.

She made life as pleasant and as normal as possible for us. Cooker and I were in the Cub Scouts. I remember a project we had called the 'Soapbox Derby.' We had to take a block of balsa wood and make a race car out of it. Mom got one of the factory workers to use the machines there to shape and streamline the car for us. It was tapered like a shoe! Mom was a special lady. She was always filled with such energy and life. She was blessed with a strong work ethic. She deserved better than Johnny. He was good to her in material ways, but he never stepped up to the plate to do the right thing, to make her an honest woman. Instead, he had her working his illegal number rackets.

When Harlem came around, Mom needed help, as this was becoming a full-time job for her, and she was juggling two jobs. Her brother, my Uncle Freddy, entered the picture, training with mom and then branching off to a separate location at 165 Christopher Street. It was the building that my friend Mikey (Door Knob) Duran lived in. Mikey was part of the Dirty Dozen so he got Freddy the apartment. Freddy went to work full-time in the numbers game. He would meet the controller, a Black guy from Harlem named Mr. Jewels, and pick up the numbers. He would also pick up at the cleaners from the other two controllers.

One problem with the numbers business is that the slips create a paper trail. Before paper shredders were readily available, they would boil the slips on the stove in big macaroni pots full of water mixed with a little bleach and then they'd flush the slips down the toilet. The whole operation was under surveillance and you could never be too careful. One day, Smilie, Johnny, and Cooker were arrested at the cleaners. When they searched our car, they found a machete in it, and they took all three of them to the 'Tombs,' which is what we called the Manhattan Detention Complex. They eventually let Cooker go. Johnny and Smilie had to go to court. They both beat the case. They had nothing on them. Not long after that, they arrested Uncle Freddy.

Gambling arrests could usually be beaten, but Freddy had a prior felony conviction for high-jacking. He got 4-to-12 years as a sentence. He served 5 plus. While he was in jail, my aunt was paid 200 a week as a way to acknowledge that Freddy did the right thing. The cops wanted him to rat but he kept his honor. I still remember the one cop, Scarantino, an Italian, who tried to buddy up with Freddy to soften him up to talk. We learned in that trial, in the discovery paperwork, that they labeled Johnny as the disappearing "Il Diavolo." Uncle Freddy got out of jail in his mid-fifties. Not long after, he died of a heart attack.

Johnny corrupted our family. He came into it and turned a normal life into a life of crime, lies, and deceit for everyone. There were always bad influences growing up in our neighborhood, of course. But Johnny didn't shelter us from the bad. He reveled in it and dragged us all into the mud with him. He may have gotten us out of some trouble when we got in too deep at times, but other than that, he pulled us into a dark side of criminal activity that damaged all of us.

He wasn't a father. He wasn't a husband. He was a presence. Mostly, he was a bad influence. Johnny's existence in our lives always reminded me of that scene in The Honeymooners when Ralph is telling Norton, "That time when you got hit in the head with a bat, who got you a cab and took you over to the hospital? I did. Who came up and saw you every day? I did. Who brought you cigarettes and candy? I did." Norton fires back, "Who hit me in the head with the bat? You did!" That was Johnny. He hit us in the head with a proverbial baseball bat and then he cleared his conscience by paying for the hospital bill. The damage was already done.

Chapter 12:

The Devil of Thompson Street

Our neighborhood wasn't ruled by the same laws that govern the rest of the outside world. We had our own ways of handling things. We had our own local government that decided right and wrong and doled out justice accordingly. The mob ruled the roost in the Village in those days. If you had a problem, you went to them, and it was settled. No one called a cop. No one ever had to. There were rarely any petty crimes against residents in the area. There were no break-ins, no muggings, no vandalism. People knew each other, they cared for their neighbors, and they looked out for one another. It's an ironic notion that when the neighborhood was controlled by criminals, there was actually less crime!

When I was young, Thomas "Tommy Ryan" Eboli was the big guy in the neighborhood. He had worked as a bodyguard for Vito Genovese. Then he moved on to being a boxing manager and represented a young fighter by the name of Vincent "The Chin" Gigante. Tommy Ryan was eventually made Capo and put in charge of The Greenwich Village Crew. The crew controlled many of the organized crime activities throughout downtown Manhattan, and some of their rackets included labor racketeering, gambling, loan sharking, hijackings, and extortion of businesses. The lineage of the Crew's leadership started with Vito Genovese, the family's namesake who ran it for nearly three decades from the 1920s to the 1950s. Anthony "Tony Bender" Strollo took the reins when Genovese was imprisoned in 1959. Then, after Tony Bender's disappearance in 1962, Tommy Ryan gained control of the family.

An urban legend in the neighborhood was that there was a mysterious stranger who used to walk up and down Thompson Street. As the folklore went, this mystical man wore a top hat, cane, and a van dyke beard. He is said to have approached several men and bargained with them. He promised them great wealth, power, and influence in exchange for their souls. Most men rejected the enigmatic drifter and his peculiar barter. But not all of them. Tommy Ryan is said to have taken the man up on his offer. He made the deal. That mystery man was said to be "The Devil of Thompson Street." Tommy Ryan made a deal with the devil. The Devil seemed to keep up his end of the bargain. Tommy rose in the mob, gaining stature and becoming the boss. Eventually, he would have to pay the Devil back.

Tommy Ryan owned nightclubs and gay bars. He controlled rackets down on the docks. He also was the owner of Jet Music Corp., which was a jukebox supplier, and Tryan Cigarette Vending Service. I was young at the time of Tommy's reign.

When I started working at the dry cleaners, it was the summer of 1968. That was the year that I graduated from Pompeii. Tommy rarely walked into the cleaners himself; he had Dominick "Quiet Dom" Cirillo bring in his clothing. Dom would become a boss himself one day, but at this point, he was a young up-and-comer in the family, not even a soldier at the time. Dom would walk the clothing over to the store. Sometimes Dom would pick up the clothes when they were cleaned, or I would deliver them to Angelina's Candy Store on Thompson Street, which was Tommy's club and hangout. Unlike other gangsters, Tommy was never stationary. He appeared to always be on the go. It was as if he wanted to be a moving target. Johnny, for instance, had a set pattern of time that he spent in his club. Johnny was a day person. Chin was an afternoon/night person. They all had a routine they stuck to. The few times that I was in Angelina's and she knew what time Tommy was coming, she would get rid of me or ask me to leave. Tommy was always seen in the neighborhood being driven in a car, always on the move, and by design, hard to pin down.

When I was hanging out at the Morosini Club, playing basketball or shooting pool, Johnny owned Tommy's bar on the corner of Sullivan and Bleecker, opposite the Pizza Box. Guys would bounce back and forth from the Triangle Club at 208 Sullivan to the bar. It seemed like they did this to break up the monotony of their days. The gangster life can be a lot of things, and one of those things, quite frankly, is boring. They are creatures of habit. The day in and day out of it all can be tedious. For security reasons, there is an unvaried way to the lifestyle — the same guys, the same places, things that you can rely on and trust. Gangsters rarely go to places they don't know or stay with people they haven't met before. Their circle is tight and their behavior is rather routine. Tommy tried to break that cycle.

Law enforcement never really got a beat on Tommy. His constant movement worked, and his unpredictability kept them off his trail for the most part. He was only locked up once, and it wasn't anything substantial. He punched a boxing referee one time inside the ring after a decision against one of his fighters went the wrong way and he got 60 days for it. This was a minor infraction for someone who lived a life of crime. People considered this more evidence of his deal with the Devil. Exoneration from all wrong-doing in this life, no jail, no punishment, but all of it to be paid back in spades for eternity.

Tommy could be belligerent and unkind when he wanted to be. I remember my mother telling me a story about him. One night, when she and Johnny were at a separate table at Jimmy Mangia's having dinner, Johnny's partner from the cleaners, Wo Wo, whose real name was Vincent Landophi, was dining with his girlfriend. In walks Tommy, and he starts to berate Wo Wo in front of his girlfriend and the whole crowd in the restaurant. Apparently, Wo Wo was late with his payment, and Tommy wanted everybody in the joint to know it. Mom said she felt so bad for Wo Wo and how he was publicly humiliated. It affected her so much that she mentioned it to me when she came home that night.

Another night, Joey was robbing a few tourists over near 8th Street around Waverly Place. It was just outside the neighbor-hood limits, and he was doing it to strangers. That was also part of the rules. Don't shit where you eat. As Joey was walking away with whatever he had grabbed off the tourists, a Cadillac pulled up, and the back window rolled down. The driver was Joe "GI Joe" Sternfeld, Tommy's longtime bodyguard and chauffeur. Tommy was in the backseat. He called Joey over to the car and snatched whatever money Joey had taken off the tourists. He told Joey, "I'm the only one who robs anybody around here." Then Tommy rolled up the window and the car drove away.

In addition to the belligerent behavior, Tommy could also be greedy sometimes. There's an old expression, "Pigs get fat, hogs get slaughtered." Tommy wanted more and more. His downfall really came when he borrowed a ton of money from the Gambino's to fund a big upstart drug operation, one that he saw as potentially making him more rich and powerful, and would legitimize his leadership role in his own family. The problem was, his drug racket crashed and burned with multiple arrests of his crew, and when it came time to pay the piper, he didn't have it. Suddenly, he was in Wo Wo's position, with the Gambino's breathing down his neck for payment.

It all came to a head one summer night in Brooklyn in 1972 as he was coming out of his girlfriend's house. As Tommy got into his Caddy, a truck drove by with a gunman in it, who shot him five times in the head and neck. Tommy died instantly. GI Joe was suspiciously not hit. It's said that the whole drug operation was a set up from the beginning by the Gambino's and the Genovese's to take Tommy down and replace him with a different head of the Genovese family. Who knows? Could be. Johnny knew, for sure, and he wasn't saying. But that is exactly what happened. Tommy was out. Funzi was in. Life went on in the neighborhood. Johnny's routine stayed the same. In the morning from 10 to 12, he would stop by 208, then head over to King Street. I never really saw a change in Johnny, or in anybody, after Tommy's demise. Right around this time, the Harlem numbers entered the picture, so maybe it helped Johnny monetarily with the turnover in power. In the end, that's all that mattered to anybody anyway.

It has been said by those in the neighborhood, the old-timers mostly and those subscribing to tall tales, that the day after Tommy was gunned down, July 17, 1972, a tall guy in a top hat, cane. and van dyke was seen walking up and down Thompson Street again, wearing a devilish grin. Word is he had come to collect a debt on a deal made many years earlier on that same street. Perhaps he was looking for another deal as well. There was no shortage of gamblers on that street. For most people in the neighborhood, all they had to bet on was themselves and their own souls, and some were willing to wager it all for a chance to live well now and pay it back later. If the "Devil of Thompson Street" was real, Tommy Ryan wasn't the only one who was willing to make a deal with him.

There were guys on every corner, in every club, down every block, who would be willing to make that same deal Tommy made, to make more money and fill the ever-shifting power vacuum in the rackets. Most of them had souls that were terribly compromised, to begin with from years of illicit activity, so to lose them completely would be a trade-off they would make any day of the week, and twice on Sunday. Tommy wasn't one of one; he was one of many. So long as men are willing to do bad, the Devil will always be there to make a deal for your soul in exchange for earthly possessions and the perception of power.

For some guys who were looking to matter in a morally corrupt world of violence and treachery, it was a no-brainer. They never believe their own day of reckoning will come. They think they're above it. None of them are. They're gamblers who think they can't lose. They always do. In deals such as these, the Devil always wins. He has to. He's playing with house money.

Grandma Angelina
Accidentally Shot and Killed in 1932
in a Mob War in Greenwich Village

Mom and Dad

Our First Set of Wheels

Stomping Ground

"Where's Johnny"

79

New Year's Eve
Mom and Johnny

Mom, Dad, Aunt Rose
and Uncle Freddy at The Copa

The Brothers with Bobby Rydell at The Latin Quarter

1972 We Are The Champions

All In The Family

Mister
"America"

Christmas on the Farm

Stormy the Horse
Dante Luigi the Donkey

Little Dante

A Cowyboy's Life is
the Life for Me! - Thin Lizzy

Family Road Trip
Rome on Segways

Practicing

Andy Serkanic
July 11, 1948 ~ January 7, 2015

"I work for God!"
R.I.P. "Bro"

Chapter 13:

Staten Island or Bust!

By 1974, things were going well for my family in the numbers business, or so we thought. The transition of Uncle Freddy to bookkeeper went smoothly, which meant Mom now had only one stressful job to work instead of two. I never counted raising Cooker and me like a job for her, but it certainly was. We were no choir boys. We were out of control. Cooker was a wayward altar boy who would drink the unblessed wine from the tabernacle every so often. We were hanging out with the wrong crowd. Although to be fair, there was no right crowd in the neighborhood in those days. As we entered our teens, it was clear that we were wayward kids. A change of scenery was needed in order to help us stay out of even more trouble.

Uncle Freddy moved out of the neighborhood when he returned home from World War II. He went to Staten Island and New Jersey, always staying close enough to the Village where his roots were and where the real action was. By doing this, Freddy believed he could have the best of both worlds: being away from the chaos of the city, and yet living close enough so that it was an easy drive by car. He became a commuter. Keep in mind, years ago there were fewer cars, less traffic, and gas and tolls were cheap. Moving out of the city meant peace of mind, quiet, trees, space, and clean air. But most city people soon realized that nothing seems quite as important when you leave the city. The city is brimming with life and excitement. It's the place where everything matters just a little bit more. For city people, the connection to the city is always there.

Uncle Freddy convinced us to move to Staten Island and live together. We found a brand new, two-family house in Eltingville. It was close to the train station, and there were commuter buses three blocks away that would take about an hour to get to midtown, which was convenient for Mom's job. Even though the commute was relatively simple, it gets old pretty fast, and it begins to wear on you, especially when you're used to stepping out of your building and being smack dab in the middle of everything.

Freddy's family consisted of Aunt Rosemary, who we called Rose, and her daughter Kathy. This was Freddy's second marriage. Both parts of the house had three bedrooms and two bathrooms. Eventually, Grandpa Marcello was rescued from the Village and had his own bedroom downstairs in Freddy's half of the house. Our half was upstairs, we each had a separate bedroom like everyone else in the house. Life was good. We were close to Rose and Kathy, having driven to Florida with them in the past on vacation. Rose was like a second mother to us. Kathy was the sister we never had. Kathy was a couple of years older than us, but it worked out very well since she had a bunch of girlfriends who were fun to be around. We would sometimes party all together in the Village. We'd come home with a couple of Dirty Dozen friends and continue the party at the Staten Island house, our new headquarters. We even had this guy up the street named Artie, who Kathy had befriended, partying with us. Our house became party central. Years later, Kathy would be the first of us to leave the island. She got married and moved back to Elizabeth, New Jersey, where she grew up.

She had been commuting to work at a hospital in Elizabeth every day while she was living in Staten Island.

The development that we lived in consisted of 8 look-alike houses built by the same upscale builder. The house cost 65 thousand dollars. The down payment was 17 thousand. Johnny lent us $8,500. Later on, we sold the house, and we paid him back, without juice!

Our house was in the middle of the development. Artie's family was on one end, and the Marino brothers were on the other. We always suspected the Marino brothers of being mobbed up just by the way they conducted themselves. We never found out for sure. We minded our own business, and had our own secrets to protect. We moved from mob neighbors to mob neighbors. Even my Aunt Rose's relatives, the Pastiche's from Connecticut, were mobbed up, and her best friend, Patsy, had a husband who was an underboss. There was no escaping it for us.

Cooker and I always had big, flashy cars, and we drove them fast. The commute to the city was an hour, but we figured out how to cut that time in half when we drove at night and on the weekends. Funny how even though the other 4 boroughs are part of New York City, we only refer to Manhattan as "the city." We would do 100 mph on the Staten Island Expressway. We drove our cars like rockets. Only God knows why we were never killed doing this. As a matter of fact, we never even got a ticket. Coming and going, to and from the city like it was our own personal raceway, we had somehow avoided having an accident, too. This would change one night while I was bar hopping on the Island.

Slowly but surely, I had developed a definite false sense of immortality. I had gotten away with everything my whole life. I committed crimes and never got caught. I helped others commit crimes. I spent most of my time around tough guys and wiseguys who always felt they were beyond reproach. When we got in trouble, there was always a way out, either through Johnny and one of his connections or by threatening somebody or paying them off. In my warped mind, I could do what I wanted on Staten Island. I was from the city. I had big shot friends. So, a little drunken bar hopping was no big deal.

The island had some nice clubs with live oldie bands like "Danny and the Juniors" who had a hit called "At the Hop" or the Del Vikings with their hit, "Come Go With Me." That was my favorite song because it began with my name - Dom, Dom, Dom, Dom, Dom, Dom De Doobie Dom! My favorite club was Crocitto's Lounge on Sand Land in South Beach. The doorman, a fellow Villager, was named Buttons. He was a little bit older than me. In this place and others, I would drink rum like a pirate. This transformed me into a pirate gangster. Except drunken pirates were on ships, not driving recklessly on Hylan Boulevard in a shiny new, 1973 Olds Delta 88. That thing had a 455 rocket V8 and 4-barrel carb. Now that was the ultimate chick magnet. I had stepped up from my old motorbike for sure. On that night, the car was a potential death rocket with a crazy pirate behind the wheel.

I misjudged a bend in the road. I didn't slow down. I fish-tailed and hit a parked car. Both cars were badly wrecked. Mine had $2,500 in damage to it. My head smashed against my side window and broke the glass. But God saved my life. I was arrested on the spot by undercover detectives riding in an unmarked car, a taxi cab. I was drunk, disorderly, and resisted arrest. This was not my finest moment. I'm not proud of any of it. When the police were done with the arrest, I was permitted to call home and they sent Uncle Freddy to pick me up. He had been drinking that night also with Mom and Rose, but he was the only one with a driver's license, so they sent him.

Freddy went to the library by mistake thinking that he was at the police station. The doors were locked so he started knocking on them. Soon he realized his mistake, drove to the real police station, picked me up, and we went home. They released someone accused of drunk driving into the custody of someone who was drunk and let us drive home together! You gotta love the 70s.

The next day we dumped this whole problem in Johnny's lap. Johnny, in turn, dumped it on Happy to fix. Those long tentacles of the mob were extended. Two assembly members were notified. They suggested a lawyer for us who was a former judge. Johnny and I visited him, and he questioned me so he could understand the case and set up a defense strategy. I answered truthfully. Johnny chewed me out when we left the office. He said, "Never be totally truthful with your lawyer because they won't fight hard for you if they think you're guilty."

On trial day, Johnny was with me, and there was a laundry list of charges against me. The cop took the stand and the DA presented the evidence. It was looking like I was dead in the water. Then it was my lawyer's turn. He stated my defense, said some legal mumbo jumbo and did some maneuvering. The judge deliberated for a few minutes, then handed down my sentence. The DA and the cop were salivating for a victory. The judge rendered the verdict: Failure to keep right, 50-dollar fine. That was it! That was my sentence. Their jaws dropped. Failure to keep right?! The crash was in the right lane! As we left the courtroom, the cop and DA looked at me with bewilderment. The looks on their faces said it all. What the hell just happened?! As we left the courtroom, Johnny paid the lawyer in cash. I'm not sure what it cost, but you can't put a price on freedom. I walked out of that courtroom scot free.

As if I hadn't gotten myself into not enough trouble, I bought a new toy to try and kill myself with. A 1967 BSA motorcycle, 650 CC, 160 on the speedometer—another death machine! I had learned my lesson: no more drinking, and driving—no more recklessness. However, I did drive the motorcycle when I first bought it with just a learner's permit. I didn't have a motorcycle license. In the summer, I hurt my back, so I would ride the bike to New Jersey using the Outerbridge Crossing and go swimming in the Atlantic Highlands. This really stressed Mom out. She hated it when I rode the motorcycle.

The biggest and worst stress for Mom and Aunt Rose was when Freddy was arrested and went to jail in 1976. I remember going on the road trips with them up to the prison in Dannemora, New York, over 300 miles away. But it was a stone's throw from Canada, only twenty miles from the Canadian border. All straight highways. I would drive 100 mph to get there. It seemed like it took forever. It took about six hours with a couple of piss stops. They would actually encourage me to drive fast. It was a torturous trip because of the miles and all of the emotions involved. It's hard to see someone you love trapped in a steel cage that way. Freddy was the second in the family to leave the island, albeit in handcuffs. Soon, I left too. I decided to cohabitate with Kathy (my future wife, not my cousin!) in Saddle Brook, New Jersey before we were married.

When I look back, I still wonder if it was a wise move to leave Christopher Street. Money-wise that apartment and building were fantastic. Great location. The rent was cheap, $300. The building eventually went condo. We should have continued to pay the rent for the apartment or transferred Freddy and the numbers operation there. Staten Island was fun while it lasted. It was never home. Only one place could ever truly be home. In the end, with Freddy in jail and me in New Jersey, Mom and Cooker went back to the Village.

Rose and Grandpa Marcello moved into a rented house near the Staten Island Mall.

Chapter 14:

Rocco

"Friends, Romans, countrymen, lend me your ears;
I come to bury Caesar, not to praise him.
The evil that men do lives after them;
The good is oft interred with their bones;
So let it be with Caesar."

~ *William Shakespeare*

Rocco Arena was the mild-mannered shortstop on our CYO Championship team. That's how I first met him. He was a quiet kid who grew up on the outskirts of the neighborhood in the Projects on 17th Street called the "Fulton Houses." It was a tough neighborhood in those days, nestled between the meatpacking district and the Department of Sanitation salt mines. It was ethnically mixed with Blacks, Hispanics, and a high concentration of Irish. This was before the area became the artsy enclave known as Chelsea. We called it "Uptown" because anything above 14th Street was uptown. Our neighborhood technically ended at 14th Street, and so too did our world. Nothing of any consequence ever happened above 14th Street. We did, however, from time-to-time, interact with kids from Uptown, like Rocco, who would come down to the Village to play ball with us.

Johnny Pettinato was everybody's friend. He was a neighborhood sports coach and an all-around do-gooder. Johnny looked out for the neighborhood kids and for any kid in trouble for that matter. He was always bringing new kids around as recruits to play on our teams. Johnny believed that athletics kept kids occupied and off the streets. Basketball and Softball were our primary sports. Rocco was one of several kids who joined our teams. He was something of an outsider. Not going to grammar school with us made his upbringing, his family, and his personal life, a mystery. Everybody in the neighborhood knew everybody else's business. We knew each other's parents and grandparents.

All of our roots in the neighborhood ran deep. But Rocco was an enigma to us. We never had a chance to vet his background. He could've been a Martian for all we knew. He didn't grow up with us. He didn't even look like us. He had thick, black, curly hair. He was a little darker and could have passed for a mixed-race kid or what we would've called back then Mulatto. Frankly, we didn't really care what he was. We were high school kids, and he was a good athlete, and we needed him to build a team to beat The Thompson Street Basketball Dynasty.

This was pre-Dirty Dozen, but most of the Dozen were never serious about joining organized team sports anyway. They played pickup games occasionally but weren't part of a team. Rocco and others were brought into the neighborhood as outsiders – mercenaries, if you will - who joined our basketball team and our championship softball team. Guys like Harry, Jay McGuire and Anthony Castellano became our teammates. Anthony was no relation to Gambino Family Boss, Big Paul Castellano. Although, one night Anthony was mugged on West Broadway and the press received an anonymous call from Auggie, always being a ball buster, stating that it was Big Paul's nephew. The dummies ran the story! That must have scared the shit out of those muggers.

Coming from a tough neighborhood into ours was an easy transition for Rocco. He was a quiet kid who played hard and played fair. He never had a problem with anybody and kind of kept to himself. That all changed one day for Rocco when he was walking across 14th Street. He got jumped by a couple of guys who tried to rob him at knifepoint. As the story goes, and it made the papers too, Rocco, who was unarmed, beat the shit out of both of them. He suffered only defensive cuts to his forearms, which required multiple stitches. He showed them off like he was some kind of fucked-up messiah with stigmata. The two guys were badly hurt. Rocco didn't have any weapon at all on him. He did it to them with his bare hands. This fight and the publicity around the fight elevated Rocco to gladiator status in the neighborhood. That day and that incident were where the legend began. It also seemed to be where his whole attitude and disposition changed, and so did the course of his life.

Not too long after the beating he gave the two would-be attackers, Rocco developed a massive chip on his shoulder. He was fist-fighting with everybody. He fought with Harry, Joey, and Jay. He punched Jay in the mouth and broke his front tooth. It's almost as if he was building an amateur street fight record to compete with the prizefighters that we would see on TV.

Rocco could fight. He had fast hands and a big punch. He should have fought in the Golden Gloves. He could've put his aggression to much better use. But Rocco didn't want to be a boxer. He wanted to be a dunsky—a tough guy. He was morphing into a punk and a bully right before our eyes. He wanted to be on the fast track to becoming a wiseguy. He would rather have had a reputation for being feared and respected than being loved and respected. His physical appearance changed as well. He started to bulk up. He had been a skinny, lanky kid, and suddenly he looked like a broad, buffed-up bruiser. In a few years time, he went from a string bean to a large beanstalk, which kind of made his head look smaller and slightly out of proportion with his body, which is ironic because he was also developing a reputation for having a big head and a big ego. He was also becoming quite intimidating.

Rocco's personality and demeanor were, as I have said of a lot of the rest of us, "type A" all the way. He was always brooding and pissed off. He looked like he could explode at any point. He was truly fearless, though, I'll give him that much. He was always throwing caution to the wind. He was also ambitious. I don't think he ever graduated from high school, and he certainly was not going to get a regular job flipping burgers. Rocco's role models were all gangsters. He looked up to the mob in the neighborhood and gangsters on TV and films. He rooted for the bad guy to win all the time. Rocco always reminded me of Jimmy Cagney in the film "White Heat," especially the final scene when his Cody Jarrett character is standing on the gas storage tank with a gun and he says, "Made it, Ma! Top of the world!" And then, the tanks explode and he's blown to kingdom come.

In Rocco, we now had a perfect monster-at-large in the neighborhood. Nature, nurture, steroids, violence, mob influence, and a bad attitude had all converged to make him a vicious, dangerous individual, the type of person you would never want your daughter to date. One of Kathy's close friends, a Bedford Street girl named Maryann, didn't read the handwriting on the wall with Rocco. She got involved with him and eventually married him. This was perfect for Rocco. Maryann was cute, sweet, loyal, and kind. She truly loved him. He seemed to love her, as well. Rocco was also attracted to the idea that Maryann's uncle was rumored to be Funzi Tieri. (Alphonse Frank "Funzi" Tieri, also known as "the Old Man," was a New York mobster who eventually became the front boss of the Genovese crime family.)

Rocco's folklore kicked into high gear as he began to make money. He started to play the part of a made-man, even though he wasn't one yet. He wore a Rolex, drove a Mercedes convertible, and sported a full-length mink coat. He was a flashy beast. He recruited an entourage. Tweet became his confidant. Tweet was part of the Dirty Dozen, but became very close to Rocco. Perry and Dino's Club became Rocco's hangout. I liked all those guys and wished that they would have stayed away from Rocco. In my eyes, Rocco had developed rabies, which is contagious and deadly.

Rocco started to commit serious, violent crimes such as armed robbery, home invasions, drug dealing, and robbing other drug dealers — some of which he did with the blessing of the local wiseguys, some without. He was on a runaway train without brakes. He had become a dangerous, belligerent bully. He enjoyed belittling guys. His favorite term to throw around was "Boy Ass." He used it to denigrate and emasculate. He'd call a guy a "Boy Ass," then he'd pounce. Or, he'd shake his fist at someone from across a room to taunt and terrorize them.

One day, I drove Lopes to see Rocco on Bedford Street to pick up the money that Rocco owed him. We walked into the club, and Tweet was there, doing his bookmaking. Rocco was in his usual scumbag mood. Lopes approached him, and Rocco took a big glass ashtray and threw it at Lopes, hitting him in the forehead. Immediately blood gushed out everywhere. I grabbed Lopes and rushed him to Saint Vincent's, our local hospital, for stitches. I was all too familiar with St. Vincent's from my own emergencies there.

Luckily, I found parking close by. Before we exited the car, Lopes handed me the money in his pocket — about ten large in cash. He was feeling faint from the shot to the head and the blood loss. Plus, he had always been anemic due to a chronic bleeding ulcer. Still, he was more concerned about someone robbing him than he was about his own personal health. That's how much he loved money. His fixation with hundred-dollar bills and bills, in general, was beyond belief. He would place them neatly in order, all facing the same way, and he exchanged old bills for new ones. He would go home and iron them on occasion. I shit you not! Lopes had OCD before that was even a thing.

After this incident, I said to myself that someone had to confront Rocco, and I nominated myself to do it. It was time to grab the bull(y) by the horns and make things right. We were all guys from the neighborhood, and we couldn't have him treating people this way. One night, while I was drinking in Jimmy Mangia's bar, in strolled Rocco and Tweet. We said hello and had a few drinks together, and I decided to broach the subject. Tweet was taken aback by my boldness because he knew what a hot head Rocco could be. Rocco and I had words. I brought up to him all the fights with mutual friends and that it was not going to be tolerated anymore. Back and forth, cursing at one another ensued. We got in each other's faces, and Tweet had to separate us. Rocco and Tweet walked out.

I was strapped that night and stayed that way from that day on. I had been issued a carry permit by the NYPD as the owner of GBA Meats, which was a cash-oriented business. My gun was like my American Express card. I never left home without it. It's that simple. An argument over street honor could lead to murder.

I never looked for trouble. I was taught to honor and respect people, and then you will be honored and respected yourself. Pushing people around just isn't the way it should be done. Slow, strategic, methodical movements on the chessboard will get you the win. Brute force is a sprint, but life is a marathon. I never liked bullies. They prey on the weak. And, in the end, street bullies are only tolerated for a short period of time. Sooner or later, they get pushed back. At this point in his life, Rocco was infected with full-blown stage-four rabies. He burnt every bridge that he crossed, never thinking that someday he might need to reuse one of those bridges. He didn't care; he got off on being a tough guy. He started to believe he was untouchable. The word was that Chin liked him. Rocco had balls. He was a willing enforcer and a good earner. He was gaining tremendous street cred. He was growing in stature.

Everybody in the neighborhood knew him. This kid, who didn't even grow up in the neighborhood, was now known to everyone by only one name—Rocco.

Rocco also ran the nightclub 'Heartbreak' on Varick Street, a block away from the entrance to the Holland Tunnel. It was a popular spot with neighborhood people and outsiders alike. Groups came to the club from other neighborhoods and other boroughs. Rocco was the sheriff in there, running the place for Sullivan Street and making sure things stayed under control—even though inside the place was completely out of control. The New York Times described 'Heartbreak' as "a school cafeteria cleaned up for the prom." Basically, it was a dance club, a 'disco,' as we used to call them, but it was also a hangout, and ostensibly, it was a drug den. This was the height of the 80's cocaine craze. The whole place, especially the bathrooms, were filled with illicit drugs. Pills, pot, and everybody's favorite, coke, flowed out of every orifice of the club.

Rocco was riding high, but he was running with a rough crowd, and he didn't see the edge of the cliff up ahead. Guys like him never do. When you're in the drug business, you deal with some unsavory characters. Then, add to that his own brash behavior, a reckless penchant for sticking up whorehouses and card games with a shotgun, and killing people in the middle of the street, and you have a deadly mix of brazen behavior and outright disrespect. There's no shortage of young up-and-comers who thought they could get away with anything. Loose cannons are not tolerated well by the higher-ups. The old school guys like Johnny, Chin, and others, wanted to keep things quiet. Flashy and boisterous only brings unwanted attention. Unwanted attention only brings trouble from the press and law enforcement. Rocco was out of control and it was just a matter of time before it all came to a head.

Years ago, Staten Island was a favorite dumping ground for the mob to dispose of bodies. That's where Rocco met his fate as well. Authorities found Rocco's body there. He was shot in the back of the head, and he had been tortured to death. It was a gruesome and violent way to die. It was also a mob message to all up-and-coming wiseguys to obey the rules.

Again, it comes back to those neighborhood rules, written and unwritten. There were many rumors about why Rocco was killed. One was that it stemmed from a problem he had with Chinese drug dealers. Others had him being set up by one of his own friends. Another suggests that the Genovese family farmed out the killing to the Bonanno family. All of those are possible. Like a lot of facts about Rocco, the exact details about his death remain a mystery. I'm sure Johnny knew. I never asked.

Rocco's death hit the neighborhood hard. He was a mainstay. Some people saw him as becoming a boss one day. People started to see him as a big shot and went to him for favors and help. A neighborhood woman had been taken advantage of at one of those wheel games at the Pompeii Feast. She lost about $40 trying to win a prize because the guy on the stand encouraged her to play more and more. She didn't win anything. She went to Rocco in the club on Bedford Street. Rocco walked over to the guy in the stand and told him to give the woman her $40 back. The guy did what he was told. Rocco did a good deed. Those actions were few and far between. Most of the time, it was drugs, guns, fights, and crime. It had to come to an end.

I didn't go to Rocco's wake. I should have gone for his wife's sake, but I just couldn't. It was an open coffin in Perazzo's Funeral Home on Bleecker Street. The entire neighborhood turned out. So did the FBI. Agents sat in a car across the street the entire time–just like they always do whenever a mob guy dies. They're not paying their respects; they're snooping.

They're looking to see who shows up and takes down names. Rocco was a guy they had their eye on, and I think, on some level, he would've liked that. He was a guy worth watching. All these years later, people still talk about Rocco. They remember him for the extremes, the extravagance, the bravado, the toughness. I'll always remember him as the kid from Uptown who came to the neighborhood to play ball with us. I'll remember him as a good shortstop who helped us win a championship. That's how I want to remember him. Not as someone who lost his life and was left face down in a Staten Island swamp – but rather, as a winner.

Human beings are the only species on earth capable of such premeditated acts of violence toward each other. Rocco's life and death were a wake-up call. It was also a cautionary tale. The evil that men do lives on; so does the good. Everyone remembers Rocco. Let him be remembered as a kid who went the wrong way, who had the wrong influences, and who couldn't be saved. In our neighborhood, we all could've been Rocco but for a parent, a girlfriend, a priest, a friend, or an event that pulled us back from the brink. Rocco lived fast and died fast. He had a mercurial rise and a terrible fall.

After his death, it became clear to all of us that leading a tough guy's life has no easy way out. There's always somebody tougher. There's always a moment when you drop your guard. There's always a price to pay. The neighborhood was no place for young men who were looking for a better life. The neighborhood mentality was a death sentence. I wish Rocco would've listened to me that night in the bar. I wish it could've gone a different way.

RIP, my teammate, my friend.

Chapter 15:

The Riot

On the evening of September 8th, 1976, a group of young men armed with baseball bats, clubs, table legs, and other weapons stormed into Washington Square Park in New York City, apparently hellbent on driving out a particular group of people from that area. During the brief course of events, several persons were attacked, resulting in homicide and injuries to many others. Were the attackers Vigilantes? Racists? Or, was there another reason for what they did? This is the true story of the Washington Square Riot.

The neighborhood was something worth protecting. That's how a generation before us had grown up. Keep the outsiders out. Keep to your own rules. Take care of your own problems. What the first Italian settlers had created in the South Village was a community governed by its own old-world mentality. They did this through their sense of duty and commitment to family and order, and of course, through their religion, Roman Catholicism, which bred a specific morality. Right and wrong were not always consistent, but it was understood by all. Even though many of the worshipers back then were Buffet Catholics-they took what they liked, a little bit of this, a little bit of that, and they left the rest — they still went to church, said their prayers, and believed in God. But the governing body which would dole out justice and settle disputes in the community wasn't local law enforcement. In the ethereal realm, God ruled. In the home, it was the father and the mother. Out on the streets, it was the wiseguys.

Italian immigrants came to America with only a few cents in their pockets but with plenty of sense in their heads. They had a sense of hard work and a willingness to assimilate to get what they needed—a job and a better way of life. They spoke little English initially, so they would do menial labor that required minimal mastery of the language: construction, shoemaking, fish mongering, haircutting. To cut hair, all you needed to understand were two words, "long" and "short."

What the Italians retained from the motherland was the value of community and a tribal sense of loyalty. They felt safer among their own, where they felt understood. Not just because of the language, but because of the customs and the belief system. America could be a scary place for foreigners. It was at once open and yet, unwelcoming. Immigration was an invitation for unskilled workers. They were needed to help build a growing nation, a necessary nuisance to be tolerated by the Anglos, the Dutch, and the Irish before them. The Italians were brought to the party, but they weren't given a seat at the table. What was not offered to them they learned to take, and what was taken, was kept. When they didn't have a church that welcomed them, they built one; two actually. St. Anthony's of Padua on Sullivan and Houston and Our Lady of Pompeii on Bleecker and Carmine. When they didn't have an area to call their own, they established it. They created a community where they felt at home with their own kind and their own traditions. Their tribal bonds, established in the old country, were now a part of daily life in the streets. Their small businesses sold specialty products that were at first only enjoyed by other Italians: fresh pasta shops, pork stores, bakeries. These businesses and their patrons became the foundation for the neighborhood. To this day, some of these places still stand and flourish in the Village—Faicco's on Bleecker, Raffetto's on Houston, and Vesuvius on Prince. These businesses are now destinations for so-called "foodies." Back then, they were Mom and Pop stores serving a community that longed for a taste of the old country.

The South Village Italians were set in their ways, and that was a quality that made them strong in their convictions, but also made them intolerant of change. They were creatures of habit in the ways that they thought and worshipped and lived. They had surrendered most of their language to assimilate publicly for the sake of work, while still speaking Italian at home. There were few accommodations made for those who did not speak English. No signs or announcements in Italian. It was English or bust. Italian immigrants learned to speak English by necessity without any formal education. They picked it up on the street. They learned the ways of their new country as a necessity to survive. They respected their new land and wanted to be a part of it while retaining their own culture and traditions. The neighborhood became a reflection of their values. It became their domain, their home. They developed a fierce devotion to it and became protective of it, sometimes in a violently possessive way.

The Italians had a good 50-year run all to themselves in the Village, where their way of seeing the world was the dominant cultural influence on the neighborhood. In the late 1950s, the bohemian counterculture movement began to encroach on the neighborhood. The 60s brought protests, flower power, free love, and drug use. Then the 70s came in and introduced to the world an illicit drug culture that infiltrated the area and threatened the safety and security that had taken a generation to create. With the advent of this drug culture, Village inhabitants such as Beatniks, NYU students, and even some neighborhood kids began buying and using drugs from the small army of drug dealers that began to crop up, mostly in and around Washington Square Park. A park that had been for families and children, students studying under trees, and pushcart vendors selling their wares, had turned into an open-air drug den — a cesspool. Brazen pushers openly solicited and sold marijuana, pills, and heroin to users. Non-users were harassed as they walked through the park. It got so bad that you could not get from one end of the park to the other without being asked to buy drugs. Police were nowhere to be found. The dealers controlled the park.

Joey had enlisted in the Air Force because of a sense of duty to country, and to get away from bad influences in the neighborhood and keep out of trouble. When he returned home with an honorable discharge, he walked through the park and was taken aback by the aggressiveness of the drug dealers. He was in his twenties, but still old enough to remember the neighborhood when stuff like that never existed. Not out in the open, at least. He was pissed off to think of the women in the neighborhood, mothers, sisters, wives, or girlfriends having to walk through there and being accosted by these predatory pushers. He thought somebody should do something about it. A lot of people in the neighborhood thought something should be done too, but who was gonna step up and do it?

There were some obvious choices about who you'd think would take control of the situation. Take these lowlife pushers and chase them out of the neighborhood. The police were not one of them. No one expected that. By the mid-70s, law enforcement had essentially given up on entire areas of the city and was reduced to advising residents not to ride the subways after 6 pm. Very helpful for those who worked nights! But the usual protectors, the ones that everybody looked to for order and justice, the so-called wiseguys, didn't seem to care. Why would they allow this garbage to go on in their own neighborhood? It was a question that baffled some, especially the old-timers who wanted to know how this could be. How could they let these low-lives intimidate and threaten neighborhood people? That's not the way it's supposed to be. But that's the way it was. Why?

The answer hurt too much for many in the neighborhood to really accept. But it was plain and simple. The wiseguys, who were respected yet feared by neighborhood people, and in some circles, even venerated, just didn't give a fuck. Because, in the end, the wiseguys never gave a fuck about anybody except themselves and what was good for them and for their pockets. That's a hard fact that people in the neighborhood had to accept. Their heroes, the ones who had cars when nobody had cars, who ate in restaurants when everybody else ate leftovers at home, and who wore fancy suits when everybody else wore t-shirts, those same guys, didn't give two shits about anybody except for themselves. The people in the neighborhood found it easy to hate the scumbag drug dealer on the corner, but didn't take the next step and ask: who put that scumbag on the corner? Who was making money off of that scumbag's sales? Whose wallet was getting fat from what that scumbag was doing? The answer was clear if anybody cared to see it. There was a scumbag behind the scumbag, and he wasn't Black or Hispanic. He was Italian. But it's hard to hate your own. Much easier to blame the stranger, the interloper, the pusher on the corner.

There's no supply without demand. If you set up a lemonade stand and two weeks later you haven't sold one glass of lemonade, you kinda take the hint. And that's the end of your lemonade business. Drug pushers exist because drug users exist. It's plain and simple. Those aggressive dealers were strategically positioned on those corners around the park and inside the park because students, hippies, artists, professors, and yes, even neighborhood kids wanted drugs. They bought drugs from them. From recreational users to stone-cold junkies, these dealers had a strong and consistent clientele. They were emboldened by their customers and the lack of law enforcement. The territory in and around the park became theirs. It was clear to Joey, and to other guys from the neighborhood that there was no justice. It was just us. And something had to be done.

It all came to a head when a drug deal involving a kid from the neighborhood went bad. This kid, Frankie, a lovable guy from Morton Street, who was what we used to call 'slow-minded,' (now he'd probably be considered autistic), had a problem when he went to cop himself some dope. As I said, Frankie was a little slow on the uptake. He was hooked on junk. I don't know if the drugs turned his brain to mush or if he was like that before the drugs, but he wasn't right in the head. He'd make a few dollars delivering groceries or helping one of the supers take out the garbage, and then quickly deposit it with a dealer for his fix. Frankie was a junkie. But he was our junkie, a neighborhood junkie. And like I said, it's different when it's one of your own.

One day Frankie caught a beatin' at the hands of the pushers in the park. They took his money, slapped him around, and sent him on his way without his stuff. Embarrassed, bruised, and desperate, he went to Joey, who everyone knew had it up to here with the park and its inhabitants. When Joey saw Frankie, poor, hapless, helpless Frankie, a victim at the hands of the dregs in the park, he blew his top.

Joey was waiting for a reason to put a hurtin' on the pushers in the park. He loathed them with an abiding hatred, "with a passion," as we used to say. He talked about it. He was fixated on it. He did everything short of actually planning his retaliation. That is until Frankie came to him with a busted face. Then he was ready to put a plan in motion.

Joey stood over the dining room table in his tenement apartment on Thompson Street. There was a large slab of paper on the table —battle plans. This sick bastard, ex-soldier, neighborhood kid, was ready for out-and-out war. Frankie's face was swollen and puffy. Joey gave him an ice pack and told him to hold it to his cheek. This would help to reduce the swelling, and also it would keep Frankie from talking. Since he wasn't all there mentally, Frankie would tend to repeat himself, especially when he was nervous. Doyle, a tough Irish kid from uptown, gripped a Louisville Slugger. Baseball bats, pipes, table legs, and sticks were strewn about the room. Heavy artillery for an ensuing battle.

Joey was ready to go that night. His fury was clouding his reasoning. There was a knock at the door, and Frankie was hoping it was Mikey, who Joey sent on a reconnaissance mission in the park. It wasn't him; it was Sanchez, a Puerto Rican kid from the Fulton Houses in Chelsea, at the door. Joey was recruiting, building an army for this fight, pulling guys from wherever he could, making unlikely allies. On this day, everybody was a neighborhood kid. It was all hands on deck. Joey wanted to take down a drug dealer named Blue. Blue ran the show in the park and was in charge of all the other pushers. Blue was the target. But he was a bad-ass motherfucker, surrounded by an army of his own - a legion of two-bit pushers who were on guard duty 24/7.

There was no love-loss between Sanchez and Doyle. Spics and Micks don't mix. But sometimes, my enemy's enemy is my friend. This was one of those times. Blue was the enemy, not tan, as Sanchez reminded Doyle. Everybody wanted to know why Blue and his boys jumped Frankie.

Frankie held fast to his story that it was Blue, and it was from outta the blue. Nobody believed that. That didn't matter anymore. This was Joey's war now. The "community" could not stand that a kid can't walk through a park in his own neighborhood without a bunch of fuckin' yoms startin' shit with him. They were gonna pay this time. Joey handed out the sawed-off table legs and the chains. Sanchez was bringing a crew. Joey was waiting on other crews from the Sixth Ward and Chinatown too. A veritable United Nations of street warriors assembled to take down Blue and his drug dealers. Frankie swore up and down that Blue was always on the west end of the park, except when he wasn't. Mikey was checking on that. Joey's plans were to seal off every entrance and exit point in the park to trap Blue and to corner him like the filthy rat he was.

The plan was for everyone to assemble at 7 p.m. on the corner of MacDougal and Washington Square South. Then from there, they would disperse to cover the eight entrance points into the park. Frankie was getting more and more nervous that Mikey hadn't come back. He was supposed to locate Blue and report back with his whereabouts. But the plans were in motion, and there was no stopping them now. They'd push into the park, 50 strong at least, and they'd get Blue and his pushers, and they'd avenge Frankie's beatin'. By the time word spread on the street, it was more like 100 guys of all ages, creeds, and colors, chomping at the bit to hit someone, most of them not really sure why. But once a train leaves the station and works up a head of steam, inertia takes over, and it pushes forward with great force and speed, requiring a much stronger counterforce to stop it.

The top of the Washington Square Arch has an inscription that reads:

"Let us raise a standard to which the wise and the honest can repair. The event is in the hand of God."

125

This event, this 'Riot,' as it was called in hindsight, was a long time coming. Things in the park had gotten so bad; the city did nothing, nobody did anything. Much like the rest of the city at the time, it had descended into chaos. Vigilantism was the flavor of the day, with films like Death Wish illuminating the problem of urban crime and the everyman's secret desire to take matters into his own hands. Vengeance was presented as a virtue. So, while the media took the case and ran with it, calling it a 'Riot and Racism,' the only thing they had right about was the first letter in those words, the "R." This incident was about revenge. Revenge for Frankie. Revenge from a group of guys who wanted the drug dealers out and wanted their neighborhood back. Another "R" word comes to mind, a Rumble. This was, in theory, a good old-fashioned rumble. Unfortunately, like all acts of violence, things usually get out of control, especially when there is a large group of people involved.

Once the gathering of guys from the neighborhood and beyond stormed the park, all hell broke loose. They bashed everyone and everything in their path. Innocent bystanders were pummeled. It was no longer a search and destroy mission for Blue and his boys, whose exact whereabouts were never confirmed by Mikey. It was a free for all. Instead of a drug dealer being hurt, a guy enjoying an ice cream cone on a warm September evening was beaten to death. It only lasted minutes, but the result was horrific. The repercussions were also long-lasting. Joey was arrested and labeled the ring leader. So were a bunch of the other guys. They were made an example of. The media ran with the story of white guys, Italian guys, driven by racism, who wanted these Black guys out of the neighborhood. The only problem with that narrative is that if racism were the motivating factor, how do you explain that the guys who stormed the park that night, were a mixed group of Italians,

Irish, Latin, Asian, and Black. That never came up in court. So, the word spread that Joey and the others were railroaded. Two years later, in 1978, the first state hate-crime statute was passed in the United States. It provided for penalty enhancement in cases where violence was motivated by prejudice against four "protected status" categories: race, religion, color, and national origin. That same year, Joey and 4 others involved were convicted of manslaughter in the first degree, conspiracy in the second degree, two counts of assault in the second degree, and riot in the first degree for their part in what was labeled "The Washington Square Park Riot."

The wrong-minded nature of the actions taken that night in 1976 goes back to a very basic misunderstanding of property. Public spaces, streets, neighborhoods, they don't belong to any single group. They're shared spaces; no one group has a right to possession over any other group. The park didn't belong to the neighborhood kids any more than it belonged to the drug dealers. Or the gays on Christopher. Or the artists on West Broadway. Or the transvestites on 8th Street. It was their neighborhood, too — all of them.

Joey and the Italians may have felt a proprietary sense of ownership, a "We were here first" feeling of entitlement, but it wasn't theirs. Just ask the Indians about being there first and how much that really matters. Their Italian grandmothers and grandfathers may have built the neighborhood, may have put their blood, sweat, and tears into it, may have made it a safe place where people would want to live and raise their kids, but in the end, it didn't matter. In the end, what did they get for it? A kick up in their ass. In the end, it wasn't theirs. It wasn't theirs to have or to protect. It didn't belong to them. They couldn't protect the neighborhood from the drug pushers any more than they could protect it from the wiseguys who allowed the pushers there in the first place or who shook down local business owners for fake protection payments. When, in reality, the only people those proprietors needed protection from was the wiseguys themselves. And no one could protect the neighborhood from greedy developers who saw a gold mine in the old tenement real estate and turned it into a proliferation of chichi luxury condos and overpriced micro-apartments. The old-timers couldn't have predicted that, any more than they could have imagined drug dealers roaming freely around their neighborhood and nobody doing anything about it. Until that one night, when somebody did. Joey and the rest of them took matters into their own hands. And then they paid the price for it.

The story of the 'Riot' grew into urban legend and neighborhood folklore, with Joey being hailed as a hero in some circles, and that he was railroaded. Put on a cross for the sin of wanting to protect his neighborhood. Maybe so. Maybe his intentions were right. Maybe he was the only neighborhood kid willing to stand up to the pushers, and maybe that stands for something. Just maybe.

Chapter 16:

Goin' Away

Mr. Rogers used to sing, "It's a beautiful day in the neighborhood." September 8, 1976, was not a beautiful day in my neighborhood. It was a dark one. It was a day that cast a heavy shadow over the neighborhood for years to come. That day in Washington Square Park, which left one innocent person dead and thirteen others injured, is a day that will live in infamy. One of those injured had a fractured skull and lost an eye. If the neighborhood guys who committed this wrong-headed act of supposed vigilantism could only have a do-over, like when we played wiffle ball and we'd argue over a foul, we could have had a different outcome. But we can't go back. We can only go forward. Nobody was supposed to die or get severely injured. There were casualties all around that day from the innocent to the perpetrators. Young lives lost or severely compromised on all sides. They say the first casualty of war is innocence. That day, in that park, innocence was lost forever.

Every action has an equal and opposite reaction. The neighborhood was often a place where bad actions had no consequences. Guys got away with many things under the protection of an insulated world, or a wiseguy using his influence or pulling a favor. What they couldn't get away with was murder, and that's what this riot in Washington Square had brought. This case would force the neighborhood and those in it to deal with issues of crime and punishment in a way they never had to before. Somebody had to pay the piper this time. Racism and retribution were the outcries from the media and the government. Jail time was the only solution that would've been acceptable, no matter who had to serve it. This case pulled back the cover the neighborhood had lived under for a long time. It took away its ability to police itself, to set its own rules and boundaries, and to dole out its own justice. This situation shines a light on what could often be a violent, unforgiving place. The Hate Crime statute was going to be applied in this case and it was going to paint the Italians of the South Village with a broad brush of prejudice, discriminatory, intolerant, and violent actions. A label that would stick like flypaper to those for whom it was true and for many who didn't have a racist bone in their bodies.

The trial lasted five weeks. The government's star witness was a 14-year-old kid, one of many kids they brought in and hounded for information. In the days following the attack, police swept through the neighborhood, rounding up every kid they could get their hands on and grilling them. Many were coerced and threatened with jail time if they didn't give up names. Some gave up the first names that came to mind, or the names of others whom people assumed were involved. Kids were scared. They talked out of fear. Witnesses in the park said they heard the attackers yell, "Get out niggers!" They also said the attackers were Italian or of Italian descent. It's unclear how they could know this just by looking at them as they quickly fled past them. But that was the takeaway from the attack. The belief was this was an unprovoked attack by a group of racist Italian youths from the Village. That's the angle the press and police propagated and pursued. In the end, they arrested ten kids, ranging in ages from 15-20, and of mixed race. They were charged with riot in the first degree, reckless endangerment, assault, and unlawful assembly.

Authorities would eventually contend that not all the attackers were white, but that at least two were Black and one was Hispanic. They concluded the incident was more of a neighborhood dispute than a racial confrontation. They acknowledged that

youths had gathered to retaliate against a Black drug dealer, but reported that as they charged into the park, "they went berserk and struck out at everyone in the vicinity." This report came too late. The charges of racism as the primary motivation stuck to both the kids and the neighborhood. Five of the ten accused were convicted. The others were acquitted. Of the acquitted, I knew one: Rocco. I've often thought if he had been convicted and sent to jail, he could possibly be alive today. God only knows. Of the five convicted, two were my dear and personal friends, Joey and Mikey.

I wasn't at the riot, though. I was living in New Jersey at that point and did not know about it until I saw it on TV the next day. It had happened on a Wednesday. Had I lived in the neighborhood still, it is likely that I would have been a part of it. The media wrote about it as being highly organized. They said it was vigilantism. The charges by the media were wildly speculative. While it would have a noble cause to do away with crime and drug dealing in our neighborhood by outsiders, Washington Square Park was a lost cause. It had been abandoned by politicians and their lack of will to take on the dealers. Police had long turned a blind eye to it all. The park was symptomatic of a disease that afflicted the city in general. It had become a degenerate cesspool of neglect. Vandalism, graffiti, poverty, homelessness, and fear were rampant.

Vigilantism became a hot topic in the mid-1970s. Rising urban crime rates across the country were fueling a bloodlust for justice, or more accurately, for vengeance. The Riot, as the press called it, came on the heels of the success of the revenge film Death Wish, which starred Charles Bronson as an ordinary guy driven to revenge after his wife and daughter are attacked and raped in a home invasion. The film was criticized by some as an example of white male rage. They found it incendiary and exploitative and accused it of advocating violence. However, the film resonated with a frustrated American public at the time and it became a hit. The Washington Square Riot fit the mold of a great racism-fueled vigilante story and the press ran with it.

My friends, Joey and Mikey, paid a hefty price for their involvement in the riot. Joey was sentenced to twelve years in prison and served six. Mikey got slightly less time. To this day, nobody knows exactly who hit who during the incident. The government had multiple informants who twisted the story to exonerate themselves or who were given deals to point the finger at others. These rats got away scot-free, scurrying back to their holes, while others were prosecuted. Joey and Mikey went to jail with stiff sentences and were publicly labeled "Italian racists." That's a bad label to enter prison with. That label alone could have been a death sentence if another inmate had wanted to make a name for himself. Joey, being short in stature, and being the ringleader of the Riot, was a target in prison. He was a good street fighter and was a survivor, but inside a prison, that's a whole new world of shit to contend with. Guys were coming out of the woodwork to attack him. They each wanted to be the one who exacted their revenge on the racist vigilante. Joey had to bulk up just to stay alive; he exercised and lifted weights. I was proud of him and his survival plan. Eventually, he was bench-pressing 350 lbs. Not bad for a guy who was 5′ 5″ and under 165 lbs.

When I went to visit Joey in jail, I would ask him to flex his neck muscles for me, just to make him laugh. They would expand, and it reminded me of the South American Basilisk lizard that runs on top of the water. On occasion, after he was released, I would ask him to flex his neck and crazy Joe would do it for me. Joey's smile and his demeanor always reminded me of Paul Newman in Cool Hand Luke. Luke's smile, like Joey's, said that nothing and no one was ever going to break his spirit. He took his sentence and did his time in the best way he possibly could.

It was hard to see Joey, a neighborhood legend, a fighter, and a champion of causes, locked up in some shithole jail upstate, and not be able to protect him. He was on his own. Prison is not melodramatic like in the movies. It's really ominous, dangerous, noisy, and smelly. If you think you're a tough guy in jail, you're in big trouble. Some prisoners just don't care about anything and have no value for life, their own, or anyone else's.

I would go on road trips with Andy, my brother-in-law, to visit Joey. Andy was another "do-gooder" in the neighborhood, always trying to make things right, similar to Joey and myself. We often got ourselves in hot water in the process by sticking our neck out and leaving ourselves vulnerable. Even the riot situation, ultimately, was about defending the honor of a fellow neighborhood guy.

Now, all prisons have a designated area for picture-taking. Polaroid Instamatics were used back in those days. The picture cost five dollars and it was taken with a backdrop that made it look like you're on the beach of a far-away exotic island. Meanwhile, you're in an upstate New York penal colony. In the photo, Joey's flashing his megawatt smile. I look pretty basic and stoic. Andy looks like he's the prisoner. This happened in every picture that Andy took with us in prison.

It didn't have to end up the way it did for Joey and Mikey. They had mediocre lawyers at best. That's all they could afford, and still, I'm sure the lawyers were not cheap. Looking back, I realized the trial was bungled. Many mistakes were made. If I were on trial, my mother would have hired William Kunstler, the famous civil rights attorney. This case was not about racism; it was about street justice. Kunstler would have made it a fair trial. This case was about getting even with the drug-dealing scum who were the intended targets.

So, Joey did his time, fighting whenever he had to, sometimes winning, sometimes losing. His main focus was to stay alive and get out in one piece, which was easier said than done. That's the way the ball bounces, no do-overs. You would think that being from Thompson Street would have helped Joey, but the media and government made this an untouchable case. Even the mob didn't want to touch it. It was too high profile.

Mikey, my other close friend, was doing his time in Dannemora Prison (the true name was the Clinton Correctional Facility in Dannemora, New York; people just referred to it as Dannemora Prison), the same place Uncle Freddy was in. Mikey lived on Perry Street, so he grew up with the 11th Street Irish Hoodlums, primarily his uncle's Hanley Clan. Mikey wasn't like them, but every so often, I would see the resemblance when his "beer muscles" surfaced. That was his liquid courage. Mikey was more of a lover than a fighter. He had a good line of shit and had many women friends. He was handsome, with jet Black hair and a slight resemblance to the actor Alan Alda, tall and thin with green eyes. One day the subject of girls came up, and being curious, I asked him, "What's the story with Andy? I know how you get your girls, how does Andy get his?" Mikey's answer was, "Did you ever see his cock? He's hung like a donkey!"

Andy befriended a rock group one day while at work. They were performing at CBGB's, and they wandered into the White Horse. He struck up a friendship with them, and they would keep in contact with us as to where the gigs were. We all figured, rock group, groupies, girls galore. By the way, they were a good group with talent, which was an added bonus. Their home base was out on Long Island. Andy, Mikey, and I were used to road trips to bars in far-off galaxies in search of new women. I was always the driver. Since I lived in New Jersey and was a manager, that required driving for the company,so I always had a company car at my disposal. Some weekends we would end up in Tattered Tom's in Upper Bergen County. That joint was not accustomed to seeing wild men like us. We would stay until closing, sometimes getting lucky, sometimes not.

On another road trip, we decided to visit Vandals on Long Island. Rides out to Long Island are long, that's how it got its name. They often referred to the LIE, Long Island Expressway, as the biggest parking lot in the world for its slow-moving traffic. Fortunately, we were traveling at night and it wasn't as bad as the daytime driving. We arrived at the venue, and within a short period of time, Mikey would reel in a girl. He'd be talking to her all night. At closing time, he'd tell us to leave him there which meant that Andy and I were driving back together.

We were both trying to keep awake with this mother of all rides ahead of us. At one point, while I was driving, I swear I fell asleep at the wheel on the Southern State Parkway for what felt like 15-20 minutes. I was sound asleep at the wheel! Andy was also asleep in the passenger seat, but I did not know this until years later. When we finally got back to the village, I slept at Andy's. For years, I thought about that ride, not really knowing what happened. Out of the clear blue sky in New Jersey one day, Andy brought it up and confirmed that he felt as I did; that angels were driving the car that night because when I woke up, I was refreshed enough to continue the drive home. That night, God gave me another pass and didn't want me to meet the Grim Reaper yet. I never found out if Mikey got lucky that night, but he couldn't have gotten luckier than we did.

Mikey and Joey had a lot in common, starting with their Italian/ Irish heritage. They both had a way about them with women and they liked having a good time. It was heartbreaking to see them end up in prison the way they did. Andy's favorite of the two was Mikey, having known him longer. My top dog was Joey. My Mom also loved Joey. Everyone did. He was a pure neighborhood kid, through and through. From his looks to his attitude to his gruff voice. For years after the Washington Square incident, the word in the neighborhood was that Joey got railroaded. Whether he was defending a friend or defending a neighborhood, Joey was seen as a hero. He grew into a legend. What happened in that park was something that the people in the neighborhood wore as a badge of honor. They believed that taking on the drug dealers who had taken over the park and stole it away from residents, was a noble endeavor. The innocents who were hurt were unfortunate collateral damage. The charges of racism were seen as nonsense. The neighborhood saw itself as Charles Bronson. Them against the world. If the police and the government weren't going to do the job, then someone, like Joey, had to. He had the balls they didn't have.

The drive upstate to see Mikey was a time to reflect on all that had happened. It was definitely a wake-up call, an education. It tattooed a message into my brain: "Be good, but if you can't be good, be smart, and don't get caught." I think jail put the kibosh on Mikey. When he came out, he worked for his uncle in the moving business, and he hurt his back. Carrying heavy furniture on his back, up the stairs in those buildings, destroyed his spine. He was prescribed painkillers, which made him slightly immobile and his weight ballooned. It was a downward spiral, the beginning of the end. Mikey died in his 50s of heart failure.

Joey went into construction when he was released from prison. We are still good friends. I will always believe he had the best of intentions when he went into that park on that fateful day. He was always a tough guy, but unlike many, he was honorable, too. People are not always the way the media presents them. Joey was a young man with a family, friends, and a desire to defend the honor of his neighborhood. Then he became the scapegoat for law enforcement, politicians, and the media. After all that they tried to take away from him, he still became a local hero. Joey was a symbol of our neighborhood: accused, maligned, persecuted, punished, and then, like the Phoenix, he rose from the ashes: stronger, smarter, and more powerful.

Chapter 17:

The DeCurtis Hit

March 22, 1988. It was a cold and quiet Tuesday morning on Bleecker Street. Shortly after 8 a.m., school children in their uniforms, bundled up in winter coats, were let into Our Lady of Pompeii a little earlier than usual to get them out of the freezing weather. They filed into the school, and their principal closed the door behind them. Steps away, Gregory DeCurtis, a neighborhood guy in his late 20s, sat in his 1984 stretch Cadillac limousine with a friend. The windows were closed, so whatever conversation they were having was known only to them.

Suddenly the roar of a motorcycle engine could be heard. The red and white bike came barreling down Bleecker Street. There were two men seated on the bike. Both of them wore black helmets with dark visors, disguising their faces. The motorcycle stopped beside DeCurtis's limousine, and one man hopped off. He pointed a .38 caliber at the window and pulled the trigger five times. The bullets hit DeCurtis in the arm and back, killing him. The passenger was unharmed. The shooter jumped back on the motorcycle and they fled east on Bleecker Street and out of sight. The gunshots brought out store owners and residents. The shooting had all the markings of a mob hit. But why? And who? The question spread through the neighborhood: Who killed Gregory DeCurtis?

An examination of the murder of Gregory DeCurtis has to begin with a look at the word Envy. Envy is described as the intense desire to have something that someone else possesses. It is one of the Seven Deadly Sins. The others are Pride, Greed, Lust, Gluttony, Wrath, and Sloth. Any one of these could be a reason for someone to be murdered in our neighborhood. I think that Gregory was killed because of Envy. He grew up in my part of the neighborhood, on the Bedford side. He had one younger sister and two older brothers. His mother was a loving, stay-at-home mom. His father and uncle were both soldiers in the mob.

Gregory's uncle was Guido "Dolls" DeCurtis, a Gambino member, who was murdered in 1977 during a power struggle in his family. His father, Ettore "Eddie" DeCurtis, was in the Genovese family and died of natural causes in 1985. Their base of operations was Cornelia Street in a small, blackened-out window storefront, which was close to the parking lot where I had all of my staged gladiator fights in grammar school. They were heavyweights in two different families, and they were involved in everything from gambling to pornography to murder. They were bad guys. Gregory and his brothers were normal kids, or as normal as you could be growing up as they did with those influences and backgrounds.

Although I was about four-years-older than Gregory, I remember him well, as we went to the same grammar and high schools, Pompeii and LaSalle, respectively. His brother, Billy, was two years my senior. He was Cooker's age. Gregory's family had a lot going for them. The brothers were very popular with the girls because they dressed well, they were tall and handsome, flashy, had nice cars, and pockets full of money. They were an old school version of The Kardashians. I mean that as a compliment! On our side of the DMZ, the DeCurtis's were treated like royalty. They were loved and respected. They weren't street bullies who preferred to be feared and respected.

Gregory was a mover and a shaker, always thinking big, starting legitimate businesses to earn a living. I'm not saying he was a saint; I'm sure if something shady happened to come along, he would consider that too. Very few guys in the neighborhood were completely clean. But with his father and uncle out of the picture, he was more vulnerable to predators and stayed out of trouble from what I could tell. Gregory ran W.G.T. Limousine Service out of his apartment on Bleecker street across from our old grammar school, Our Lady of Pompeii. The other corner was a restaurant called Grandpa's Bella Gente, owned by Al Lewis, the actor from the old TV show, The Munsters. Yes, Grandpa Munster, the affable and ambitious Dracula character who lived in the basement in that show, was an entrepreneur in our neighborhood.

I used to see him often outside his joint, smoking Italian cigars, "De Nobili," aka Guinea Stinkers. The funny thing about it was Al Lewis was a Jew, so apparently, you don't have to be Italian to smoke a Guinea Stinker. There was a commercial on TV years ago about Levy's rye bread. The slogan was you don't have to be Jewish to enjoy Levy's Bread! Lewis became a fixture in the neighborhood, and an honorary Italian because of the popularity of his restaurant.

Bleecker Street was a Little Italy unto itself in those days. Grandpa's restaurant was kind of a tourist trap, to be honest. It was popular, drawing a crowd because of Lewis's notoriety as an actor. He had also become a kind of bon vivant, a man about town. He was a real character. He never met a camera he didn't like. He would stand on the corner of Leroy and Bleecker, happy to be recognized and to greet passers-by and pose for a photo. All around him on the street were real, long-standing Italian establishments, like Zito's Bakery, which was Frank Sinatra's favorite bread. Sinatra used to have loaves flown to California for him when he was out there.

Then there was John's Pizza, which made one of the best pies in the city with lines that stretched around the corner. Faicco's Pork Store had been there a century. Ottomanelli's Butcher Shop was a staple. Then there was Rocco's Bakery, which was right next door to Bleecker Street Bakery. Bleecker Street was a strong Italian American enclave with businesses that had been there for a generation or more. It was a place where people knew each other and knew the businesses and business owners. It was familial and familiar to everyone in the neighborhood. It was not a place where anonymous gunmen shot someone dead at 8 a.m. on a random Tuesday. That is until it was.

Gregory was 29 at the time of his murder. He was running his limo business all on his own. He was the sole driver, and it was predominantly a night-time business for him. That meant he was networking on the club circuit throughout most of Manhattan and in the Village. New York City comes alive at night, especially in those days, the 1980s. Clubs were king. People were bouncing around until 4 a.m. and beyond almost every night. They needed a way to get around. This was way before Uber. Your choice was to call a yellow cab or call a car or limo service. It was a vibrant time and action was everywhere. There were many opportunities that could fall into your lap if you were street-wise and savvy. Plus, for Gregory, people knew his uncle and his father. They were gone, but not forgotten. They had a big influence in the club business.

Guido "Dolls" DeCurtis had a hidden interest in many bars, restaurants, and after-hour clubs, including many gay bars in the 60s and 70s, such as the infamous Stonewall Inn on Christopher Street. The Gambino and the Genovese families had shared interests in a lot of the gay bars in Greenwich Village and some uptown as well. Gay Bars and

The Mob might seem like strange bedfellows, but they really weren't. It was business. The State Liquor Authority (SLA) wouldn't grant licenses to gay bars. So, the mob found a way around it, as they always do. They established these places as "private bottle clubs," which were not in the SLA's jurisdiction. Another way around it was to convert straight clubs which already had liquor licenses to gay bars. This gave the mob controlling interests in these places which they maintained as lucrative businesses for many years. So, Gregory knew his way around the club world, and through the reputation of his family, people knew him.

One of the clubs Gregory visited on a regular basis was Heartbreak, the nightspot that Rocco ran, over on Varick Street. Gregory was well known to everyone in the club and would park his limo outside. It didn't take long for Rocco to start his bullying. As the story goes, Gregory and Rocco had words, which eventually led to a fistfight. The exact topic that led to the fight is unclear; there are many versions. The club was loud and the incident was messy. Some say it was simply about the limo being parked in front of the club. Rocco didn't want it there. Gregory wasn't moving it. Some say it was over a girl that they were both fooling around with. That could be. Or it could've been over envy.

Rocco was a kid from the projects who grew up with nothing and felt that he was earning every bit of the money, power, and reputation he was gaining, all on his own. He saw Gregory as a kid who grew up on his family's reputation. He saw him as a kid who had it all handed to him. Rocco was resentful and begrudging of such ill-begotten respect, and he was out to prove who the real tough guy was. That could be the likely cause of the fight too. Whatever the real reason, the fact is, Rocco and Gregory had a conflict that night in the club. It was one that would lead directly and indirectly to both of their deaths.

Rocco was rough. He could handle himself. There's no question about that. But sometimes drugs and alcohol and rage can inhibit your ability to think straight and to fight. Plus, Gregory was a big kid, 6' 1" and in good shape. They went at it, and Gregory got the better of Rocco. Guys jump in and break it up. This was a total mind fuck for Rocco, losing a fight in his own joint? And to Gregory, no less, whom he viewed as an illegitimate tough guy. This was totally devastating to him. Envy turned to anger. Rocco couldn't let this go. He wanted revenge. He went to Sullivan Street to ask Chin for permission to hit DeCurtis. This is where it gets complicated. Some say Chin refused to allow the hit over what was a personal dispute and because of Gregory's family history.

This was definitely a possibility. Hits bring unwanted attention. They should be done only as a final recourse, not as a first option. Chin was still reeling from Gotti's hit on Castellano outside Spark's Steakhouse, which infuriated him, and threatened to bring an avalanche of law enforcement and press attention to the mob. The last thing Chin wanted was another hit in his own neighborhood. If Chin said no, then that means Rocco proceeded with the hit all on his own. A definite no-no. He was a hot-head. His ego had been damaged. He wasn't going to take no for an answer. Rocco wasn't gonna let this go.

It needs to be understood that Chin liked Rocco. He liked him a lot. He had given him carte blanche to operate in the neighborhood, to run card games, to sell drugs, and to partake in whatever other kinds of mischief he was involved with. Chin let Rocco walk around like he owned Bedford Street, even though he wasn't born there. Rocco did what he wanted, with impunity. He was living under Chin's protection. But that protection can only go so far in their business. There are rules. Here we go, back to the rules again! When those rules are broken, the price is a heavy one. Rocco was a strong up-and-comer. Everyone knew it. He was rising and rising fast. Gregory was no threat to that. Gregory was doing his own thing. But for an incident in the club, he would have been nothing more than an afterthought to Rocco and certainly no impediment to his rise.

But envy is a powerful motivator, as is anger. In business, you don't and can't take things personally. Rocco made this personal. Too personal. And he was going to have the last word. Or was he?

On that fateful, frigid morning on Bleecker Street, Gregory DeCurtis died right at the scene. The guys on the motorcycle got away with no one identifying them because of their helmets. Law enforcement never charged anyone, nor even arrested any suspects. Rocco was immediately implicated by those in the neighborhood. He was the likely suspect. Some theories said he was the shooter. Some said he was the driver of the motorcycle and that the shooter was an assassin brought in from Italy for the hit. Some say Rocco stood across the street in front of Zito's Bakery and watched the whole thing. Whatever it was, there were few who doubted Rocco had a hand in it. And if he did, that meant he may have done it in defiance of Chin. Something that no one could survive. Rocco got his revenge.

But in killing DeCurtis, he sealed his own fate. Less than two years later, Rocco was also gone. No one knows exactly why Rocco was killed. There were any number of reasons and theories. The DeCurtis hit was one of many. It was also a peek into another aspect of the neighborhood mentality. Envy and anger can lead to violence. In the end, two more lives were lost.

The Gregory DeCurtis murder, just like Rocco Arena's, remains unsolved to this day.

Chapter 18:

God Bless America Meats

Long before Arby's struck gold with their catchy, ubiquitous slogan, "We Have the Meats," Andy and I were in the meat business, and boy, oh boy, did we ever have the meats. We had a great business and plenty of laughs. My relationship with Andy goes back many years. We were family through marriage, best buddies, and business partners. We called Andy 'Mr. America.' His surname was Serkanic. His birthday was on July 11, but he preferred to celebrate it a week earlier, on the "birthday of our country," July 4th. This was an awfully patriotic gesture for someone who looked the way he did when we first met.

I met Andy in 1974 when we were dating the Gallagher sisters. When I walked into his apartment, he was in the middle of the living room with an oversized pair of scissors in his hand, trimming some guy's beard who was sitting in an antique white, porcelain and red leather barber's chair. The guy getting the trim looked like the mountain man "Grizzly Adams." They were both smoking pot, and Andy was hacking away at this guy's beard with confidence as if he were doing a good job. He wasn't. It reminded me of a scene out of one of those Cheech & Chong stoner movies. Andy still looks like a hippie leftover from the Woodstock Festival days (which he had attended!). He was 5' 5" and 165 pounds with long hair in a ponytail and a Fu Manchu mustache. He wore thick eyeglasses, and he had several tattoos. His nose was pushed over to one side from being broken in a bar fight years earlier. He lost the fight because he was drunk, and the guy was much bigger than him. He eventually got even one night, kicking the shit out of the guy and sending him to the emergency room. So, with Andy's nose out of whack like that, it altered his voice. He sounded like a deep-throated neurotic parrot. And believe me, I know from parrots because I owned a talking African Gray, and Andy's voice sounded just like him.

Come to find out that the guy in the barber's chair getting the bad beard trim was an old hippie friend of Andy's named Bob. Everyone called him Grandpa. Andy gave him that nickname because Bob looked much older than he was. I was around twenty-years-old at this point, which means Andy and Bob were in their mid-to-late-twenties. These two guys had already lived a lifetime with their hippie adventures, from the festival in upstate New York to living in California. Andy was already the bartender and manager at the White Horse Bar when I met him, and his apartment was in the same building, directly above the bar. He continued this for several years, and when he had enough of the drunks and the bar lifestyle, he left and started a job with a meat delivery service across the street from the bar on Hudson Street.

Now, picture the same hippie-looking cartoon character that I described, but also add in the visual of him in a full-length white meat apron that, by the end of every day, is completely bloodstained. He looked like something out of a Smurf's horror movie! Andy liked this type of work, and he explained to me the business aspects of it. He wanted to start his own business. I decided to help him.

At this time, I was working on 47th Street in the New York diamond district with Charlie and Lopes. I was their unofficial bodyguard, and I explained Andy's meat business idea to them. By a stroke of luck, which Andy often had, they decided to lend him seed money to start the business. The loan was interest-free. They weren't going to juice him. That was like hitting the lottery for him. All he needed was a decent van that was refrigerated. Once we found him one, the next step was a landline telephone number and a beeper/pager. Cell phones were not available at this time. Beepers were the cutting edge of technology. You received a page to the beeper that you wore on your waist, and the number that was trying to reach you would light up. Then you found a phone booth and returned the call to that number. Annoying by today's standards with cell phones, texts, emails etc., but that's all we had back then, and we made it work. The final thing that Andy needed was a catchy name for the business. This is where "God Bless America Meats" was born.

He named it. Being that Andy's nickname was "Mr. America," the name of the business was basically God Bless Him. And Andy could use all the blessings he could get! He went one step further and had the truck painted by hand with giant flowing American flags on both sides, a giant bald eagle on the hood with the name "Kate Smith" spelled out as a tribute to her for singing the song "God Bless America." Andy loved the Yankees, and they played the song during the 7th inning stretch at every home game. Now he's a cartoon character who is driving around in a cartoon van!

You had to love Andy. He was a nut, for sure, but his meat business was an instant success thanks to his Polish work ethic and determination, along with his dynamic personality. He used to say, "Meat's my life!" He soon paid back Charlie and Lopes and started to live a better life for himself. Now, customers had his pager, or they would call me at our jewelry booth on the second line that we installed exclusively for the meat business. I would pick it up and say, "GBA Meats, how can I help you?" As the business grew, Andy befriended a guy about our age in the market. His name was Joe Solar. He was a tough Puerto Rican from Washington Heights. He was an ex-Marine and an ex-con who fit right in with us.

Apparently, Joe caught his wife in bed with a Dominican guy and may have killed him. I never really inquired further. All I knew was he was a hard worker, respectful, ex-military, and a bit neurotic like Andy. He had a penchant for parrots and owned multiple birds. He was hired, and we added another truck. It was done up just like the first one, except on this one the hood said "Irving Berlin," the composer who wrote the song "God Bless America." We gave Joe an alias. We called him Bodega Joe, because of his ethnicity. Joe didn't mind. We were up to two trucks and two drivers. Our next expansion was renting a storefront. We ended up renting one on 10 Morton Street, a quiet block with parking, and in close proximity to Bleecker Street.

My friend, Tony the Barber, had a business there called "Cafe Capri." His place was open to the public, but it was also a hangout for wiseguys. You could drink a coffee, have a vodka, play a number, borrow money, play cards, and if you were a wiseguy friend of Tony's, he would give you a haircut and a shave. Yes, Tony was a licensed professional barber, but he also chalked up about 19 bookmaking arrests in his lifetime. What a man. This guy watched over me like he was my father. Tony's sister, Lina, and her husband, Frank, were the building managers. They lived there and rented us the store. They also rented an apartment to Ed O'Neill, who played Al Bundy in the sitcom Married with Children.

I did all the construction myself in the store. We bought a walk-in refrigerator and an expensive, artistic, neon sign for the front window. Andy liked some girl that had a neon business, so we were multitasking by hiring her for the lighting. Andy always "liked some girl," and they were all knockouts. He was always a hopeless romantic, falling in love constantly. We were rocking and rolling with a legitimate business. I applied with the NYPD for a full-carry gun permit. You had to jump through hoops to get one. You had to have a clean record, safety training, and conduct business transactions with high amounts of cash. Cops only want other cops to carry guns, for obvious reasons.

A typical day for me as the coordinator or manager for the operation included driving Joe's truck back and forth to work, so we didn't have another vehicle in the street all day to watch. Joe would meet Andy at the market. They would load up Andy's truck and separate the deliveries in front of our store. During the day, as more orders were called into me, I would send them to either Andy or Joe, depending on who was available at that time. Joe would return the truck at the end of the day. During the off-peak hours, I would hang out next door or walk a few blocks to Johnny's club and hang out there. Either way, I was with my friends in my neighborhood. Lunchtime was fantastic, having my choice of food right down the block.

I've been involved in a bunch of businesses, both legitimate and illegitimate, in my day, and to be perfectly honest with you, they all suck the life out of your body. It seems to me that legitimate businesses are harder to control. There's always some idiot who's in charge who doesn't know you or your reputation, and they test your will. We had a variety of customers and different types of eateries ranging from hamburger joints to elegant, high-end restaurants. Andy got really excited one day when I designed a booklet with a cover that had images of barnyard animals on it. We had a mission statement on the first page that started with "There's nothing more American than what American's eat." I mailed this to the infamous

Fraunces Tavern, which was located at 54 Pearl Street. The place had been in operation since 1762. The location played an important role in history. It served as headquarters for General George Washington. They read my booklet and asked us for a sample piece of dry-aged steak. When Andy heard the good news, Mr. America flew sky high like a bird — like the bald eagles on the trucks and the eagle tattooed on his forearm. He was giddy over the whole thing.

On the other hand, some customers would hold up payments, which caused a negative cash flow. Then there were some knuckleheads

who jerked you around so much that you needed to cut off their credit and deal with them COD (Cash on Delivery). If they didn't pay their balance, you'd have to break their windows or their legs. One guy frustrated me to the point that I went out one night and broke all of his windows. The next day, I walked into his place unannounced, and I was acting sympathetic that someone had broken his windows. He had a bodyguard with him because he thought that the Italian restaurant up the block was mob-connected and did the job. Little did he know that I was his worst nightmare. Before I left, he paid me, and I never did business with the deadbeat again.

One day some guys stole Andy's truck from in front of the store. He had left it idling. They jumped in and took off. He saw this and took out his 357-magnum hand cannon and ran after them. In his bloody meat coat, Andy took off running down Bleecker Street, midday, screaming, and waving his gun. The truck went straight toward Carmine Street and made a left on 6th Avenue. Andy tried to cut down Cornelia Street so he could catch the thieves at the red light on 4th Street. They got away. Meanwhile, people had called the cops, reporting seeing this guy in a bloody meat coat brandishing a gun. The cops caught up with

Andy. He told them the story, and he gave them the description of the truck. They put out an all-points bulletin and about half an hour later, they caught the thief, going through the midtown tunnel. After all, how could you miss this van! The cops returned the van, undamaged with all its contents. The case was open and shut; the thief was convicted.

Andy cheated death several times. One Saturday morning, he called me. I was living in New Jersey, and he asked me to drive him to Mt. Sinai Hospital. He was complaining about his stomach, saying it was on fire. He never told me how serious it was. I went over to his place about an hour later and he was in bad shape, pale as a ghost. While driving to the hospital, he was weak and almost fainted. I was driving like a maniac, speeding through lights and so on. We got to the emergency entrance. Andy needed a wheelchair; he was too weak to walk. They rushed him in, and he nearly bled to death with an ulcer. He only had about 4 pints in his system. They immediately gave him about 6 pints and operated on him. The next day when I went to his apartment, his bathroom looked like a bloody crime scene of puke and shit.

I always felt that Andy and I were blessed with some kind of divine intervention. Andy eventually got married again and moved out of the neighborhood to New Jersey. It seems as if everybody ends up in New Jersey eventually. One afternoon after work, he was in a convenience store and started to feel lousy. He rushed out of the store, had a heart attack, and died on the pavement. A cop arrived and zapped him with a defibrillator. They rushed him to the hospital for open-heart surgery and he was in a coma for a couple of days. He stayed in the hospital for about three weeks. Toward the end of his hospital stay, he told me that when he was dead, he went to hell and saw the devil, who is purple and grotesque. This scared the shit out of him. From that day on, he had a morbid fear of death.

Eventually, the doctors installed a defibrillator in his chest, and when it was triggered, it literally knocked him off his feet. Andy soon had to give up the meat business. It was too dangerous for him to continue working. He went on permanent disability and retired. And so the run of 'God Bless America Meats' ended. Andy sold his remaining customers to someone in the market. Eventually, everything goes down. That's life. That's gravity.

Chapter 19:

47th Street

From 1981 to 1984, 47th Street in the midtown diamond district was one of the most dangerous, treacherous locations on Earth. The reason for this is simple and can be summed up in one word: money. Some places have the Crème de la Crème of society. This area had the scum de la scum. The diamond district would have corrupted Mother Teresa if she had spent any length of time there. If it did not steal your soul, it could snatch your life in a split second. My mother used to say, "Money is just a medium of exchange." Think about it; you don't own money, you just exchange it for goods and services and then go out and make more of it. Money was God on 47th Street, and it turned people into devils.

People were running around on 47th Street between Fifth and Sixth Avenue with fistfuls of hundred-dollar bills, 80lb. silver bars, gold and diamonds, Rolex watches, millions and millions of dollars being exchanged every day. It was not controlled by any one mafia family. It was wide open to everyone. It was the Wild, Wild West. You could buy anything there from A to Z. It was Sodom and Gomorrah. Everything was out in the open to see. Uniformed cops were there patrolling but to no avail. Corrupt retired policemen were holding down the fort as security guards. You had to be armed to safeguard what was yours.

I thought these guys we're faking it and that they were possibly gathering info for a large dragnet one day, but apparently not. They were hired guns to help protect businesses. Drugs and poverty were the catalysts that fueled the greed there. Junkies were stealing to satisfy their habits. Clothing from stores was lifted and resold, as was art, oriental rugs, appliances, tools, cosmetics, ceramics, and crystal. Everything and anything you could think of was stolen and resold. You could even place an order, and if possible, they would steal it and get it for you. All of these thieves were called "boosters." Then there were the desperados, the chain snatchers, the strong-arm violent criminals. All the jewelry they stole ended up on 47th Street.

There were items on the street taken during home burglaries from around the entire tri-state area that ended up here: jewelry, silverware, coins, cameras. There were hundreds of buyers on the block with no city or state guidelines to follow, no ID, and no paperwork to fill out. No city inspectors were walking around. The block was loaded with loan sharks from all the families. Speed was the Genovese representative. His real name was Fred, his brother Walter worked for Johnny and Jimmy Nap. The buyers needed a lot of cash to operate, and the loan sharks kept them flush with money. Raymond and Charlie were loan sharks also.

It was a kinetic environment to be around in the beginning, but it quickly sickens and perverts a normal, healthy human being. One day, some junkie was trying to sell her baby. I will never forget that as long as I live. I had seen some hardcore stuff in my time; but that one took the cake.

47th Street was one of the diamond capitals of the world. Innocent people would come there to buy their engagement rings. They never saw the dark side, the cesspool that it really was. Raymond and Charlie were running a gold-buying booth at 55 Exchange and brought me up there to work for them for added protection. Charlie could handle himself in a fight, but Raymond was a goofball. So, they figured I could help them, and I did.

In the 1980s, the US economy went wild, the CD rate skyrocketed, gold and silver spiked, and the stock market raged like a California wildfire. When there is more money in circulation, people buy more goods. The 80s were all about flash and glitz. A big part of that was jewelry. 47th street was making a killing. The Wild, Wild West was occupied by all five families in New York, plus the Philadelphia mob, South Jersey, and Atlantic City groups. There was a gold-buying booth directly across from our gold-buying booth. This group was responsible for the regime change of Philadelphia boss Angelo Bruno. Consequently, some of their top guys were murdered by the mob Commission, gangland-style. They were tortured and killed with bills stuffed in their mouths, signifying that they were money hungry. Meanwhile, I was there in the middle of all this, trying to help protect my two close friends and their business while trying to stay alive myself.

The booth we operated out of consisted of one showcase and a two-compartment safe with a workbench on top of it to conserve space, and two large signs that said, "We Buy Gold, Diamonds, and Silver," in bold letters. The size of the booth was 35 square feet, 5' by 7' in dimension. The rent for the booth was $2,500 a month. A guy walked up to the booth with an attaché case one day. He opened it up and showed us over 100 carats of small diamonds and some other stones. Charlie looked at the diamonds and quoted the guy a price. Meanwhile, this guy, who called himself Jake, was carrying a gun, and he wanted us to know it. That was nothing new to us. Eventually, I got a gun permit myself to carry legally. This guy, Jake, was trying to impress us with some name dropping about the Gambino family. Every other knucklehead up there was mobbed up. Jake wanted too much for the diamonds and he walked away.

It was clear that Jake was on a fishing expedition all day on the street, trying to get the highest price for his stones. He was jumping from one booth to the next, playing everybody. We knew it. There were no secrets on 47th Street. We knew all the top players. The next day we saw Jake again, and he stopped by the booth, and Charlie made a deal with him. He showed us the diamonds again, and we verified that he did not switch the stones. He was standing outside our booth with the attaché case, and Charlie told him to wait there, and that we needed to pick up some cash to pay him. He put the case down on the ground next to his legs. Bad move! Charlie had pre-planned a major sting on this guy if he should come back, and, of course, he did come back. The people next to us and around us were all in on it.

They created a diversion while someone lifted the attaché case right out from under Jake. This was an unbelievably risky and unlikely way to snag the jewels from him, but it worked. He was screaming and cursing and threatening everybody with retaliation and waving his gun around at us. He never called the cops or his mob friends. Jake was a bullshitter, and what he got was 47th Street justice. Everybody got paid on that score, including me. I got $800 for my end of it. I bought a Japanese Akita for myself with the $800 and named the dog Brando. I lived in Paterson, New Jersey, at that time, and sometimes even I needed extra protection. Brando was a lifesaver, and a home saver. My house was the only one on the block that never got robbed thanks to Brando. Good dog.

Raymond had a girlfriend named Barbara. She was a real piece of work from Fort Lee, New Jersey. Raymond was introduced to her through a mutual Jewish gangster friend named Mac Levine. Mac was dating Barbara's mother, who was also named Barbara. Go figure. These two Barbara's were grifters, always looking for a Sugar Daddy. Mac knew the score. He was over the hill, around 75 years old, and Barbara was 50. Mac was no fool. Raymond was a jerk. Mac knew he was being played, but figured he was lucky to be alive at his age, so he didn't mind being a Sugar Daddy. Mac went way back to the prohibition era with the crazy Jewish mobsters like Meyer Lansky. Even at his age, you could see that he did not back down from anybody. He would fight if he had to.

He was a loan shark who was also into bookmaking and sports fixing.

Raymond, on the other hand, thought he was in love and showered the younger Barbara with stolen clothing, stolen jewelry, and bought her a two-seater Mercedes. We warned him, don't put the title in her name. He did it anyway. He was gaga in love with this grifter. So, as predicted, they eventually broke up. Raymond wanted the car back. She said no. So, Raymond and Charlie stole the car. And they accomplished this task at my wedding to Nina, although it didn't distract from the celebration at all! But they didn't have the title. Raymond wanted the title. He negotiated with her and settled on a $20,000 figure. Then came Charlie, and another sting was planned and put into action. This plan involved the ole' switcheroo.

The two Barbaras are mobbed up because they probably sucked every mobster's dick in the Tri-State area. This mother and daughter duo thought they knew some people. Big deal. In our neighborhood, the motto was always, "Who cares who you know!" Barbara didn't want to meet us on 47th Street, so she said she was sending a wiseguy to pick up the money. He would also give us the title. Before the wiseguy showed, Charlie set up two envelopes: one with 20,000 dollars in it, one stuffed with paper. The guy showed up. Charlie counted the money in front of him on the counter. The guy was on one side of the counter; Charlie was on the other. Charlie counted out $20,000 and put it in the envelope, but fumbled it as he closed the flap. He dropped that envelope on our side of the counter, onto the floor. Charlie picked up the identical envelope with the paper in it and handed it to this so-called wiseguy. The jerk did not reopen the flap and look. Instead, he put it in his pocket and walked out. The story does not end there.

After the scam went down, it turned out the guy did have some friends downtown on Sullivan Street. The guys at 208 did not like Raymond because he always operated without a rabbi or permission. Charlie's father was friends with Ralphie and gave Raymond and Charlie fatherly advice. He said, "Give it back, or there was going to be a sit-down." Raymond sucked it up and gave the cash back. It was not worth the effort. They would have broken Raymond's legs if he did not give back the money. Charlie's father saved them. They were knocking down crazy money, so returning it did not hurt Raymond in any way. Just a life lesson and a minor setback.

Every mob family had its representative on 47th Street. One day, Brooklyn Jimmy introduced us to 'Jimmy the Gent,' the real guy played by Robert DeNiro in Goodfellas. Brooklyn Jimmy was famous on 47th Street. He was a big diamond fence and handled big-time scores. The 'Jimmy the Gent' meeting was no big deal. We said hello, shook hands and said goodbye. Business as usual, nobody impressed anybody. After a while of being on the street, you become numb; everybody is like 'The Walking Dead.' Brooklyn Jimmy ended up getting convicted for the murder of his own wife. I don't know if he did it, he was always nice to us. Another guy who would come by our booth was George Persico, nephew of 'Carmine the Snake' and cousin of 'Allie Boy Persico.' He would come by and do business with us. George was a nice guy. He looked like his uncle but was not a made man. Another tough guy named 'Little Joe' would visit us. He was a serious and intense guy. No nonsense. Very respectful, we liked each other, and we had the same demeanor about us.

There were ways of carrying a gun on the street, especially on 47th Street. An ankle or hip holster was fine. But the best way for the fastest access was to keep it inside a newspaper that's folded in three. This creates a disguise and also a pocket where you can reach-in and quickly pull out the pistol. This was important if somebody had the drop on you with their gun, and you couldn't make a move quickly enough with the gun in your waistband or ankle. The newspaper camouflaged the carry and looked harmless, but you could make a fast grab for it with two hands or you could fire it through the newspaper and no one would see the gun. The noise could still be heard, of course, but you could drop it to the floor as a decoy. I think I invented this! You were kind of safe on the main part of 47th Street. As you went home, leaving the street and going to the garage for your car, you were at risk. So, if the gun was in your hand at all times, you were much safer and could pull it out quickly to defend yourself. I want to add that this was a different time and a different place back then. New York City was different and so was the world. I'm not in any way advocating this behavior. I'm simply describing what survival was like in a world full of outlaws.

The business grew rapidly. There was a lot of money coming in. Raymond and Charlie expanded. They had a private apartment upstairs to conduct larger transactions out of the view of law enforcement. We also formed a corporation, DRC (Dom, Raymond, Charlie) Jewelry Corp. The office was across the street on the second floor. It was a place that was safer than the apartment. It had an area separated with bulletproof glass. So, if you did not know or trust the person you were dealing with, they stayed outside, and you dealt with them through the window opening. The side I stayed on was comfortable with a TV set, sofa, and bathroom. At times, if nothing was going on, it was very boring. The corporation office was more secure than the apartment. The only advantage of the apartment was convenience. Sometimes convenience will make you lazy, and in this business, lazy can make you dead.

Raymond and Charlie were set up professionally. They were leading the market on stolen jewels and gems. That meant dealing with some unsavory characters. A lot of business was transacted in the apartment. Burglary rings of criminals from the tri-state area were coming in. We would go upstairs with them. Another precaution we had was that we'd meet them upstairs, make the deal, leave the jewelry upstairs and pay them downstairs at the booth. This way, they couldn't set us up and rip us off. The only thing they could do was kill us, but with no money on us that made little sense. Also, Charlie would take off his $10,000 Diamond Rolex and leave it at the booth before conducting business upstairs. Charlie ran the show because he knew and grew the business. Raymond was a nickel-and-dime con artist. Charlie was the brain. But Charlie fucked up one day.

It's a day I will never forget! I survived that day, thank God, but I don't know how or the reason why. We went up to the apartment with two guys that we really didn't know very well. They walked up to the booth and flashed Charlie a bag of gold jewelry and said they wanted to go upstairs because the cops were watching them. Charlie should have given them the rules about no money upstairs. He didn't. He had done business with them once before, and he let his guard down this time. He messed up. We went upstairs with them, and they pulled their guns first. They got the drop on us. We were in trouble. They handcuffed us and robbed us. From Charlie, they took all his money and his watch. From me, they got a few bucks and my heavy gold chain which had a diamond crown Christ's head on it. They gagged us by stuffing some rags in our mouths and then we figured they were going to leave. They didn't. They decided to put pillowcases over our heads and pretended that they were going to execute us. Big pussies, they never pulled the trigger! That was a mistake by letting us live.

When they left the apartment, we were able to leave also, but we were handcuffed. We were very embarrassed walking around with handcuffs, but we were alive at least. Charlie, who was always a quick thinker, had a friend who was a locksmith about three blocks away. We had to walk to the locksmith to have us released from the handcuffs. We never saw the guys who robbed us. I was the most violent in our group. I was prideful and wanted revenge. I did not pray to Benjamin Franklin like Raymond and Charlie. I prayed to a God of vengeance. I was prepared to scour the entire city for some street justice. Charlie and Raymond talked me out of it. They paid me for what I lost in monetary value; to them, it was the cost of doing business. Their mentality was that sometimes the scammers get scammed. My take on this was that I wanted revenge, fast and final. Sometimes you just gotta cut your losses.

Some pimp drug dealer who looked like Gumby would hang around the exchange, all dressed up, loaded with flashy jewelry on. He actually looked like a cross between Gumby and Urkel, the character from the TV show 'Family Matters.' He wore glasses, a short haircut, and he had false teeth. Charlie, on occasion, would buy from him or sell him jewelry. One day he convinced Charlie to buy 3 ounces of coke from him. So, they set up a date for Christmas Eve to make the deal. The day came, and it was snowing, and we had to drive to Bedford Stuyvesant in Brooklyn to do the deal. Who the hell buys drugs on Christmas Eve!? We weren't even drug dealers; we never bought drugs before. Now we're trusting Gumby with our lives. Meanwhile, I had a date with my future wife to go to her parents' house for the traditional Christmas Eve meal of The Seven Fishes. Somehow, we survived this stupid move and I made my dinner date with her family. It's a good thing they did not ask me how my day went when we were at the table eating dinner.

In the building that we operated out of, which was 55 West 47th Street, there was a whorehouse on the 6th floor. Raymond was not only in love with hundred-dollar bills, freshly ironed, and neatly stacked, but he developed an everyday habit of going upstairs to get a $20 blow job. Every single day just before lunchtime, he'd head up there. He treated prostitution like it was a routine coffee break. The greed, the exploitation, the dehumanization, the violence, were all on display on 47th Street. The street was a disease, and if you stood around it long enough, you were infected. It was incurable. After almost losing my life to it, I had had enough. The robbery shook me up. It made me realize that I had been dancing too close to the fire for too long. I wanted something more out of life. I was out of there. After thirty years in street life, I had gotten my wake-up call. I was done.

Chapter 20:

Satan's Asshole

When I separated from Kathy, she moved out of our apartment in Saddle Brook. That put me back on the bar trail in the city. I returned to hitting my old haunts like the 'White Horse' in the Village. Andy was the bartender and manager there. The bar and buildings were owned by our brother-in-law, Eddie Brennen, who was married to Mary Rose. Andy separated from Helen, and Eddie separated from Mary Rose. We blew it big time with the Gallagher girls. We all suffered failures in our marriages. Oh well. Shit happens.

Eddie's partner was Jimmy Munson, who was an associate, loan shark, and Irish gangster. The group of regulars in the White Horse were usually enjoyable enough and respectful to drink with and have a few laughs. The place brought in a mixed crowd with struggling artists and out-of-work actors. Every so often, you'd even see a celebrity. A limo would pull up, and out came Robert Vaughn or even Mick Jagger. Monday through Friday, I spent a lot of time there.

Saturdays, I went to the club on King Street. I went back so they wouldn't forget my face, but more importantly, out of respect to Johnny. I felt it was my duty to go drop in. Part of it was also therapy. King Street offered me a chance to watch and learn and there were always a whole lot of dysfunctional situations to observe and have a laugh over.

You can't buy those life lessons. There's no school on earth that offers classes in what I learned first-hand in these joints.

One day when I was at the White Horse, I went up to Andy's apartment which was above the bar. I had a set of keys to let myself in. All of a sudden, from the other room, out popped this little cutie. She told me her name was Candace Martinelli, that she was from Texas, and was a singer. With that, I went down to the bar where Andy was working his regular day shift, and I asked him, "What's the deal with this Candice?" He told me she wandered into the bar like a stray cat one day and told him some sob story that she was down on her luck and needed a place to crash.

Andy, being good-natured, let her stay. He had found himself in her position many times in life and he was sympathetic to the situation. So now we found ourselves in a kind of threesome if you will. Not sexually, but all three of us were spending time together and we both were starting to enjoy her company. Andy wanted to try to advance her singing career. He knew a promoter named Niles Siegel who he'd met at the White Horse. He thought maybe the guy could help her. Niles got her a gig at the Lone Star Cafe at 61 5th Avenue on May 8th, 1979. Niles had some industry scouts there and this was supposed to be her big shot at stardom.

We prepared Candice for this day. I went shopping with her and even paid for her outfit and haircut. The night of the performance, her former boyfriend was there, the actor Judd Hirsch from the show 'Taxi.' The performance went exceptionally well, and I thought she was headed for success. I even asked her to autograph a picture for me. At that point, everything was platonic with Candice. I liked her, she was fun to be with, she was a singer, and cute, and I even liked her name. So I asked Andy, because I was always mindful of the rules, whether I could make a move on her. He gave me the okay and said, "Go for it, bro," and I did.

Now, here's where the story gets dark. Danny "Spawned From Satan's Asshole" Hanley was one of the Hanley clan. He had a brother named Terry, who we called CI (Crime Incorporated) Hanley. He also had a brother, Timmy, who hung out with us on Bedford in the club and Dodgers Bar. Timmy was friends with Jerry Vaughn because they were closer in age. Timmy was the more sensible Hanley. All the Hanleys were Mikey Andriani's uncles. Mikey was a Hanley on his mother's side. Danny had disappeared without a trace.

But Terry was the Hanley I had a problem with. He was an annoying, belligerent piece of shit with a bad reputation and a long prison record. He claimed to be connected with the Westies. With all this attention that Candice brought to the White Horse, Terry decided he wanted to hone in on her because that is what jerkoff bullies do. They push the limits, they become aggressive, until they're pushed back against. Terry started to pursue Candice openly. He was obnoxious and crude. He would use the Irish pick-up line, "Hey babe, sit on my face and I'll guess your weight." I couldn't stand him. He made me very nervous. When I got nervous, I was moved to action.

What were my options? Should I shoot him in the head up close with a pistol or shoot him from a rooftop across the street with a scoped rifle? I even thought of using a crossbow because it's silent. Either way, this bastard has got to go.

A couple of days went by, and Andy was getting nervous also. He knew that Terry wouldn't let up. He was a vulture. He was all over Candice like flies on shit. And he knew I was going to do something to stop him. It was a precarious situation. I had to be smart, but my blood was boiling. If I killed a Hanley, I was going to have a big problem on my hands. My emotions were getting the best of me, and my trigger finger was getting itchier by the second. I figured my best bet was to run it by Johnny, and get his permission to kill Terry Hanley.

I started thinking, what if this low-life owed one of the neighborhood shylocks money? If I off him, do I have to pay his debt or go to a sit-down and have a bigger problem for taking him out without a go-ahead? Pride and impulsivity is a dangerous combination and can make a small problem an even bigger one.

So I decided to go and see Johnny and explain the situation. He knew how serious I was. He knew that I carried a piece all the time and that I was ready. Johnny paused for a moment and he told me, "Don't do anything; we'll take care of it." When Johnny said, "we'll" take care of it, I knew it would be handled. Johnny went to Chin, and Chin sent word to Terry that if he continued his bullshit, he would disappear, just like his brother Danny did.

The problem was solved. Terry never acted up again. He backed off Candice and never confronted me with whatever warning he received from 208. Terry never knew how close he came to death. That's how it goes sometimes. A guy is marked for death, but certain circumstances arise and he isn't killed. I personally believe that God had bigger and better plans for me. If I had whacked a low-life like Terry, I would've hurt myself more than I would've hurt him. I would have gone to jail, or be on the lam, or I would've been looking over my shoulder for some Irishman to shoot me as retribution. My own kind could have even been forced to handle me and put two in my head. Johnny might have been told by Chin to take care of it. Sometimes, you were told to kill your own if they stepped out of line. Killing a degenerate like Terry Hanley would have been justified. It also would have been the stupidest thing I have ever done.

As for Candice, when she left Andy's and went out on her own, she somehow got involved with Hiram Isola, the pot king from Carmine Street. Hiram ruined her. The pressure of not making it in the music industry got to her, and she ended up on drugs.

Fast forward years later, Andy called me and told me "Our friend died."

I asked him, "Who? What friend?"

"Terry."

"Terry Hanley? Get the fuck outta here! How?"

Andy tells me, "Throat cancer!"

I said, "Wow, throat cancer."

Andy said, "Yeah, he got it suckin' on Satan's Cock!"

Chapter 21:

Change of Heart

My Momma didn't raise no idiot. After the stick-up on 47th Street and that brush with death, I smartened up. I put a plan into place when I realized how insane and dangerous that one city block was, and moreover, how crazy my whole life had been. I decided to make a change. Johnny had labeled me "the brain" because I was always thinking. All kinds of thinking, even negative thinking ("stinkin' thinkin'"). It was time for me to think long and hard about a way to leave the street life of crime that I had known for so long, and start a normal life.

I had given a regular job a chance in the past. Prior to working on 47th Street in this bodyguard job, I held down two management jobs in the banking industry. It was time to go straight — no more shortcuts, no more easy money, no more violence. It was time to grow up. Another catalyst for change was marrying Nina. I didn't want to mess up this marriage like I had my first one. Nina was an innocent Jersey Girl from a good family. She deserved for me to be on my best behavior. My own mother warned Nina by saying, "Are you sure that you want to marry him? He's a great guy, but..." That's exactly how my mother phrased it. This time, I was determined to do the right thing, make an honest living, have a happy marriage, children, the whole nine yards.

Being exposed to street life for over twenty years is a tough habit to break. If you have a daredevil, adventurous personality, too much normalcy can be toxic to your system. Boredom can set in. You need action. So, I conducted my lifestyle similar to someone with a split personality. During the daytime, I was in the village in the meat business with Andy, and at night I was back to New Jersey playing the role of husband and father. In 1986, my son Nicholas was born. I had a good run with GBA meats, the most fun I've ever had in my working career. I owe it all to Andy, Mr. America, for bringing me on board.

Andy surprised me one day for my birthday; he bought me a used red Cadillac from a friend in the meat market. The car was in great shape. It was another chic magnet, but I was married, so I could only dream of chicks in this ride. I was committed to honesty and loyalty. In 1987, I left GBA; the business wasn't making enough money for two partners. I had a family and needed to earn more. Andy was gracious enough to buy me out. Our accountant put a price on the business, and Andy made monthly payments to me. He never missed a payment.

I was always looking for an adventurous career in my life. Years ago, I applied to the NYPD. At that time, everyone had the same idea, and it was difficult to get in. The city was broke, the Vietnam War was over, and the waiting list was too long. I applied to the CIA. I went down to the World Trade Center, filled out the application, and never heard back from them. My secretary at one of the corporate jobs I'd held convinced me to apply for a modeling career. I took some headshots. She sent them to all the top modeling agencies. In a nice way, and so as not to shatter my fragile ego, she gently told me that the response was negative. In essence, they would say, "tell that head case to throw away his headshots!"

I decided to start a totally new career in construction. I know what you're thinking. Construction is a front for more illegal activity. And that's usually true. But not in this case. I was always interested in the field. From the time that Charlie and I had our little hang out in his basement, which we converted from a shower room, I had developed an interest in construction. We did all the construction by ourselves. We were just kids. There were three hardware stores close by that we would go to and utilize their knowledge. We combined their advice with our own ideas and, by trial and error, we would get the job done. I also built the meat store and Charlie's book store on West 4th Street. There were also other construction jobs that I worked on like the Bedford club and the dry cleaners.

I had done some projects as a hobby, but I needed to learn how to do the work professionally. I decided to get a job in New Jersey as an apprentice to learn the business. The starting pay was eight dollars an hour. I was 33 years old, married, and owned a house. My boss thought I was nuts to work for that amount. But I didn't. For the first time in my life, I wasn't interested in making a quick buck. I wanted to do something that would set me up for long-term stability. I needed the experience so I could move on. I did so rather quickly. I decided to work for another contractor and advanced my pay as I gained experience.

Eventually, two major events came my way in 1993. One was from God; my daughter Vanessa Rose was born. The second was, I was able to start Nicholas Construction Corp. I was 39 at that time. I still had energy in me to enter into another business venture.

Slowly but surely, the commitment, hard work, and new-found responsibilities took hold. Gone were the delusional days of chasing quick scores and easy money. It was a chase I had been on my whole life, and I never caught up. This was a serious awakening. It was sobering, literally.

A change of philosophy also brings with it a change of habits, like excessive drinking, which I no longer did. I put a lot of effort into my personal betterment, my family, and my new company, Nicholas Construction. It finally paid off for me. The more you put into life, the more you get out of it. It's a simple rule. For a guy who was used to following some rules and breaking others, this was one rule to live by. I was a changed man. It was so miraculous, almost as if God, with his divine intervention played a role in it.

1993 brought some amazing things into my life, and it also took one amazing thing from me–my mother. Mom passed away on April 26th, 1993, just a few months before my daughter was born. They never got to see or know each other. That was the toughest time of my life. Losing my mother tore me apart. She had been such a source of love and light and strength. It was hard to exist in the world, knowing she was gone. Another loss that 1993 brought was Johnny's death. We had drifted apart. He and my mother had been estranged for about ten years. She dumped him for lying to her. She finally got smart. She was better off without him—just as she was better off without my father. Mom never had luck with men, even with her sons. We drove her crazy. But the love and commitment we had for each other were true and deep. I was lost without her. Life was never going to be the same without Mom. The one thing that gave me the strength to survive losing her was the birth of my daughter, Vanessa. I had to keep it together. I had to be a father.

Chapter 22

You Can Take the Kid Out of The Neighborhood...

The final scene in *The Godfather Part III* has an elderly, lonely Michael Corleone sitting in a chair in the courtyard of Don Tommasino's villa in Sicily. In flashbacks, he is reminiscing about all of the important events in his life. He is remembering the good times and wondering where the time has gone. Michael was on top of the world, and his greatest regret (aside from having his brother Fredo killed!) was that he never took the time to realize all that he had in his life--most important of which is family. It all passed him by in the blink of an eye.

Being a thinker myself, and having gotten a little older and a little wiser, I will sometimes sit in a chair on my horse farm and reminisce about the past. Yes, I have a horse farm! I woke up and smelled the coffee over thirty years ago and changed my ways, and it led to all sorts of things in my life that I never dreamed were possible when I was younger. It was a true blessing that I made this change in my life so that I wouldn't die a lonely old man filled with regret myself. I built a future for my family, and I had a lot of help from my wife, Nina, who has always been by my side. As my company grew, we had a similar vision of what we wanted to do with our lives. I had found my soulmate on this crazy journey called life. We weren't interested in a flashy lifestyle, with jewelry and expensive cars. Instead, we wanted to send both of our children to college and be able to pay for it. That way, when they graduated, they would be debt-free. After we accomplished that, we wanted to upgrade from our little lakefront house to buying raw land where we designed and built a beautiful home, including that 10-acre horse farm. This was Nina's dream her whole life, and now that I was domesticated, I began to adhere to that old theory, "happy wife happy life." It took a few years to build this dream property. It was challenging, but my experience in construction helped immensely.

We had a difference of opinion about the building of the farm with one town official who was telling us that his jurisdiction superseded the state guidelines, which was incorrect, so we challenged his authority. This created a war with verbal retaliation in both directions and a tit-for-tat stance. The only problem I had was that the town had deep pockets and didn't fight fair. One day they tried to shut down the project. We had a site meeting by my foundation pit, which was essentially a large potential gravesite! As this knucklehead official started verbally flexing his muscles and threatening me, telling me how powerful he was, I could feel the old me coming back.

Years earlier, a jerkoff like that would've been cracked in the head with a rock and buried, or bashed and made to look like a landslide killed him. Then we would call for the rescue squad. Handling things violently like a tough guy is a default position when you grow up in the neighborhood. It's like a knee jerk reaction. "Who do you think you are?" is the immediate response. That's usually followed by a threat of your own and then showing the person exactly who YOU are. My instinct was to pummel this guy. Thank God that thought passed, and I didn't react violently.

We finally overcame this hurdle, which cost me about 20K in lawyer fees and aspirin, and we finished the farm project. When we were done, it was animal heaven. We had two parrots and a parakeet inside. Their names were Enzo, Pete, and Kiwi. Our outside friends were four barn cats for mice control, ponies, horses, and two miniature Sicilian donkeys. We had two structures delivered from the Amish country in Pennsylvania, a three-stall barn, and a giant shed that we used as a tack room for all the saddles and gear. We soon ran out of space, so I had to construct several additions on both structures.

To offset the cost of this operation, we decided to start a business that Nina could run. It would entail riding lessons and horsemanship. We hired a professional trainer part-time and made a go of it. We also provided horse vaulting training. Vaulting is basically acrobatics on horseback, not as intense as you would see at the circus, but it had an element of danger. Nobody ever got seriously hurt on our property. Nina did break a finger one day, though. Horseback riding is like skiing; eventually you're going to get thrown off or banged up. We had animals coming and going with the business. There I was, a kid from the neighborhood, and I'm running Noah's Ark!

Horses are majestic animals. From the beginning of time, they were owned by royalty and were a status symbol. Nina's favorite was Ripple, a beautiful, spotted paint horse who was quirky. She would make a face and play with her tongue to amuse you. Ripple had bad feet, cracked hooves, and eventually, we had to sell her. Stormy was lovable, excellent to ride, and a dream come true. Then there were the two miniature Sicilian donkeys we bought as babies. The male was Dante Luigi and the female Tullia. We gave them Italian names. These little ones were the size of a Great Dane, and they were full of piss and vinegar, always getting in trouble. I could relate to that! If you walked in the pasture with them, they would sometimes come up behind you and bite you on the ass. They even annoyed and bullied the fully-grown horses. It's funny to see them rule the roost; they're on the top of the pecking order. And that little son of a gun, Dante, all he wanted to do all day was chase Tullia. He finally caught her and succeeded in impregnating her. The donkeys were incredibly cute but also quite mischievous. The last pet that we purchased was a sweet 16 birthday present for Vanessa, a female Maltese/ Shih Tzu whom we named Cannoli. She became a dear beloved friend of the family.

The progression of our property buying was the house in Paterson, New Jersey, then the country lake house, and when we were done on the lake, it was the horse farm. Our ultimate dream was to own a home in a foreign country. My motto in life has always been "think big or go home." Nina shared this sentiment. Every vacation we went on was a two-fold mission, rest and relaxation, and a recon mission to see if we could buy a second home there.

We visited North Captiva Island in Florida. We saw most of the Caribbean islands. We loved all the vacations but did not feel that these areas were a place to build a home. As Dorothy said, "there's no place like home," and our home was the motherland, Italy! We love our Italian heritage, our roots, Southern Italy, specifically Calabria. My ancestors were from this region. It's only a stone's throw to Sicily where Nina's ancestors were from, a short ferry ride across the straits of Messina, a half-hour ride.

Our first visit to Italy, six of us went: myself, Nina, the two children, Nicky and Vanessa, Nicky's fiancé Meghan and Vanessa's best friend growing up, Kristen, whom I call by her middle name, Lucy. Our mission was to find a property to buy in Calabria--visit Rome for the cultural finale to the trip.

We had a ball—four young people and us two old farts! We saw all of the famous sites in Rome. We also went on tour through the streets of Rome on Segway scooters. This was very dangerous. In Italy, the pedestrian doesn't have the right of way, and neither does the Segway. The Italian driver is very passive-aggressive; they always seem to be in a hurry to go nowhere. It's called Mario Andretti syndrome! We found a property in a small complex, similar to a townhouse, except they call it a beach club. I became international. I had two beautiful views. From the front, we could see the ocean about one thousand feet away. The back view had farms, mountains, and olive trees. The town was ancient and yet was still active as a small fishing port. The natives were very friendly and happy to see that Americans lived nearby. They treated us like rock stars, especially when we told them we were Italian Americans from New York, and our ancestors were from Calabria. We made several friends, and they watched our property when we were not there. Calabria became a place to enjoy homemade wine and reminisce about my life experiences. I was a million miles away from where I grew up, and yet I was home. To this day, when I am in Italy, I never want to come back.

My immediate neighbors are all foreigners to Italy who also use their properties as vacation homes. They come mostly from Europe and as far away as Russia. We are the only Americans. We all get along and try to communicate in broken English or broken Italian. We also have neighbors from England. Close to our home is a family-owned food store where we enjoy shopping. The owner's son, Dominick, who runs the store, speaks English. He has tried to teach me some Italian, and we often laugh during these brief sessions. Italy, in general, is a safe place to live. The government is stable. My town has about five thousand people living in it.

One night, after dinner, and driving home on this dark roadway, the old me resurfaced. Someone driving behind me was tailgating my car. Being it was a small roadway, I slowed down to a stop and gave the idiot the finger while screaming obscenities at him. The guy knew I was nuts, and he did not inflame the situation, he simply drove around me and took off. This could have been my first international brawl! It's remarkable how close to the surface my old volatile self is. You can take the kid out of the neighborhood, but you can't take the neighborhood out of the kid.

Unlike America, the government and the Mafia have an unwritten agreement. They are in lockstep with each other. One day in my town, I saw what the Mafia did to a guy who broke the rules. Apparently, this guy made a living shooting pool. He obviously screwed up in some way, and they cut off most of his fingers. The mob is different there; you have to be a blood relative to join. They are vicious and will kill anyone, including prosecutors and judges. It's not like in the old neighborhood where they congregate in social clubs. They're scattered about in all the cafes that are everywhere. Italy is big on coffee and bottled water; nobody drinks water from the faucet. It has too many minerals in it and is bad for the body, or so they tell me. I think it's a Mafia scam to sell bottled water! I wish I had thought of it! And just like back home; they control the garbage industry. Some things never change.

In the 1900s, my Italian ancestors from this area of Italy left their country to seek a better life for themselves in America. Over a hundred years later, I came back to Calabria, seeking my ancestral heritage and to find peace of mind. It's been quite a journey. From the rough streets of Greenwich Village to the rugged coast of Calabria, life has taken me full circle. As I think back on it all, I often ask myself if I would change anything. Then I remember that there are no do-overs. It took thirty years for me to slowly evolve into the person that I am today. Now I'm the new and improved Dom. I owe it all to my mother, my wife Nina, my children, and the guiding hand of God, which seems to have always been there, getting me out of even the tightest bind.

Printed in Great Britain
by Amazon

20861186R00106